LB 2331 .
Mastascusa,
Effective instruction for
STEM disciplines

P9-CKY-330

MHCC WITHDRAWN

Effective Instruction for STEM Disciplines

Effective Instruction for STEM Disciplines

From Learning Theory to College Teaching

Edward J. Mastascusa
William J. Snyder
Brian S. Hoyt

Maryellen Weimer,
Consulting Editor

JOSSEY-BASS
A Wiley Imprint
www.josseybass.com

Copyright © 2011 by John Wiley & Sons, Inc. All rights reserved.

Published by Jossey-Bass
A Wiley Imprint
989 Market Street, San Francisco, CA 94103-1741—www.josseybass.com

No part of this publication may be reproduced, stored in a retrieval system, or transmitted in any form or by any means, electronic, mechanical, photocopying, recording, scanning, or otherwise, except as permitted under Section 107 or 108 of the 1976 United States Copyright Act, without either the prior written permission of the publisher, or authorization through payment of the appropriate per-copy fee to the Copyright Clearance Center, Inc., 222 Rosewood Drive, Danvers, MA 01923, 978-750-8400, fax 978-646-8600, or on the Web at www.copyright.com. Requests to the publisher for permission should be addressed to the Permissions Department, John Wiley & Sons, Inc., 111 River Street, Hoboken, NJ 07030, 201-748-6011, fax 201-748-6008, or online at www.wiley.com/go/permissions.

Readers should be aware that Internet Web sites offered as citations and/or sources for further information may have changed or disappeared between the time this was written and when it is read.

Limit of Liability/Disclaimer of Warranty: While the publisher and author have used their best efforts in preparing this book, they make no representations or warranties with respect to the accuracy or completeness of the contents of this book and specifically disclaim any implied warranties of merchantability or fitness for a particular purpose. No warranty may be created or extended by sales representatives or written sales materials. The advice and strategies contained herein may not be suitable for your situation. You should consult with a professional where appropriate. Neither the publisher nor author shall be liable for any loss of profit or any other commercial damages, including but not limited to special, incidental, consequential, or other damages.

Jossey-Bass books and products are available through most bookstores. To contact Jossey-Bass directly call our Customer Care Department within the U.S. at 800-956-7739, outside the U.S. at 317-572-3986, or fax 317-572-4002.

Jossey-Bass also publishes its books in a variety of electronic formats. Some content that appears in print may not be available in electronic books.

Library of Congress Cataloging-in-Publication Data
Mastascusa, E. J.
  Effective instruction for STEM disciplines: from learning theory to college teaching / Edward J. Mastascusa, William J. Snyder, Brian S. Hoyt.
      p. cm. -- (The Jossey-Bass higher and adult education series)
  Includes bibliographical references and index.
  ISBN 978-0-470-47445-7 (hardback)
  9781118025925 (ebk)
  9781118025932 (ebk)
  9781118025949 (ebk)
   1. College teaching. 2. Effective teaching. 3. Learning. I. Snyder, William J., 1941- II. Hoyt, Brian S., 1963- III. Title.
   LB2331.E41 2011
   378.1'25--dc22
                                                    2011002096

Printed in the United States of America
FIRST EDITION
HB Printing 10 9 8 7 6 5 4 3 2 1

The Jossey-Bass Higher and Adult Education Series

Contents

*We dedicate this book to our parents,
families, and all our students.*

Foreword

When I first read this book as a manuscript, I was impressed. Here was a group of engineers willing to say that teachers in the science, technology, engineering, and math (STEM) disciplines ought to be looking at the research on learning and implementing it in their classrooms. They deliver this message clearly, unequivocally, and with compelling logic.

They aren't the first or only ones to point out the need for change. In a review of the research on active learning, Joel Michael (2006) of the Department of Molecular Biophysics and Physiology at Rush Medical College writes

> As scientists, we would never think of writing a grant proposal without a thorough knowledge of the relevant literature, nor would we go into the laboratory to actually do an experiment without knowing about the most current methodologies being employed in the field. Yet, all too often, when we go into the classroom to teach, we assume that nothing more than our expert knowledge of the discipline and our accumulated experiences as students and teachers are required to be a competent teacher. But this makes no more sense in the classroom than it would in the laboratory. The time has come for all of us to practice "evidence-based" teaching. (p. 165)

Engineers are precise and systematic, and these authors are no exception. They move through the research carefully, explaining in readable prose what has been documented and what those who teach in these disciplines ought to do about it. The changes they advocate are sensible and doable. The authors write cognizant of the realities of higher education—increasing class sizes, students not as well prepared as they once were, and students beset with pressures that often diminish the time and energy they can devote to study. They write knowing about those aspects of instruction teachers can control (like when and how to use PowerPoint) and those beyond their control (like the configuration of the rooms and labs where they teach). They also write with the voice of experience. They have tried the changes they recommend, and they are willing to admit that some of their first attempts were not as successful as subsequent ones.

It is unusual, but highly appropriate, in books on teaching and learning to hear the voice of experience coupled with careful study of the literature. The book then becomes what Michael calls for in his quote—a description of what "evidence-based teaching" looks like in the STEM disciplines. The description of teaching laid out in this book is encouraging because, although it calls for change, many of the changes are not all that radical. For example, these authors point to research documenting that taking an exam can be a significant learning experience. That requires faculty to reconsider the design of exam experiences and help students see their learning potential beyond how many points exams are worth. In another chapter, based on research, they recommend against telling stories when presenting concepts. Anecdotes may interest the students, but stories can distract and muddle the mental models students need to be creating. They offer sanguine advice illustrated with examples showing how problems currently assigned can be reformulated and used in problem-based learning activities. After reading the book, it's hard to understand why more faculty aren't making the changes consistent with research findings.

You will find this an eminently readable book. It makes educational research understandable—no small accomplishment, given that educational research, like research in so many of our fields, is written to inform research more often than practice. The authors write with voice—you can hear them talking, you can tell that they're college teachers themselves. They make their way through the topics in a conversational style with an occasional interjection of humor.

It is a book written by engineers who imagine that learning can be built much like the structures and circuits they construct. Even though learning construction may not be quite as definitive as electrical engineering, teaching can be designed so that it more directly and systematically promotes learning. This book shows how that happens and how to make changes in your teaching to better facilitate learning for students.

Maryellen Weimer
Professor Emeritus, Penn State University

Reference

Michael, J. "Where's the Evidence That Active Learning Works?" *Advances in Physiology Education, 30, 159–167, 2006*

Preface

Think back to when you were a new college professor—or ahead to that time if you are just starting. You have just finished your PhD, have accepted a teaching position at a college, and are about to face your first class. What do you do?

If you are like most other new professors, you reflect on what your professors did best and try to emulate those moments. That's the way it's usually done, and it's been done that way for hundreds of years. Spence (2001, pp. 12–13) said, "Plop a medieval peasant down in a modern dairy farm and he would recognize nothing but the cows. A physician of the 13th century would run screaming from a modern operating room. Galileo could only gape and mutter touring NASA's Johnson Space Center. Columbus would quake with terror in a nuclear sub. But a 15th century teacher from the University of Paris would feel right at home in a Berkeley classroom."

Think about that for a moment. Medieval peasants are an earlier version of today's farmers, who need to know a fair amount of chemistry and biology. If they don't know the pH of their fields and the concentration of nutrients and fertilizer, then it is hard to succeed. Farmers need to know enough biology to comprehend, for example, the life cycle of crop pests, or else failure is likely.

In the same way, modern physicians cannot succeed without understanding a large amount of biochemistry and biology. Modern astronomers and space scientists need a large store of knowledge about relativistic physics and mechanics, for starters. And anyone in command of a nuclear submarine needs to know an awful lot about nuclear physics and oceanography.

But what do college teachers need to know? Currently, we seem to assume that expertise in the discipline is sufficient and that it is not necessary to be aware of how people learn. We appear to believe that the knowledge amassed in educational psychology and cognitive science in the last quarter century or so can be ignored. In all those other fields—from farming to running a nuclear sub—the person in charge receives an education that includes background knowledge necessary for job success. But universities continue to hire faculty who have no awareness of the learning process.

In education we tend to do things the way they have been done—which is what makes Spence's (2001) idea simultaneously humorous and painfully true. Most college teachers teach the way they were taught. There is no requirement that a teacher in a college actually know anything about teaching or the relevant research in fields like cognitive science and educational psychology. Particularly distressful are comments like the following:

> The preparation of virtually every college teacher consists of in-depth study in an academic discipline: chemistry professors study advanced chemistry, historians study historical methods and periods, and so on. Very little, if any, of our formal training addresses topics like adult learning, memory, or transfer of learning. And these observations are just as applicable to the cognitive, organizational, and educational psychologists who teach topics like principles of learning and performing, or evidence-based decision-making. (Halpern and Hakel, 2002, p. 37)

> Most current approaches to curriculum, instruction and assessment are based on theories and models that have

not kept pace with modern knowledge of how people learn. They have been designed on the basis of implicit and highly limited conceptions of learning. (Pellegrino, 2006, p. 3)

So, most importantly, college teachers need to be grounded in basic knowledge about how people learn. That is what we try to share in this book. This book presents and then explores a model for the learning process. The various parts of that model are based on findings in the cognitive sciences and educational psychology. For the most part, those findings come from work in the last 50 years as psychology has moved away from behaviorism to a mostly constructivist approach. Those findings together give a coherent picture of what takes place in the learning process. In examining the model, we can identify various instructional practices that aid student learning, thereby increasing effectiveness in the classroom. All three of the authors are experienced both in the practice of engineering and teaching engineering. That gives us a design perspective. In other words, we are accustomed to using basic knowledge in the sciences—buttressed by mathematical analysis—to inform the designs that we have produced. As engineering educators, we require our students to learn a vast amount of material in physics, mathematics, chemistry, and other basic sciences. Then, in the latter part of our curricula, we focus on getting students to apply that material to designing various items that have a purpose.

In science and engineering, if there is knowledge available we try to use what has been discovered in other fields (like physics and chemistry) when we design various devices. What is known about learning should be applied in the classroom similarly, and it should not take as long as it has taken in the past for that to happen. Application of basic research results happens dramatically faster in many other branches of science, and it seems rather peculiar that it has taken this long for those of us who teach—particularly in science, technology, engineering, and mathematics

(STEM) disciplines—to begin to move basic knowledge in these relevant fields to the practice of teaching.

The essence of engineering is design. In the process of design we apply knowledge from the areas of physics, mathematics, and various other sciences to produce a result. To us, it makes sense that course design and the design of classroom activities should implement knowledge from the areas of cognitive science and educational psychology to produce instruction that more effectively promotes learning. As we devised workshops involving course design, we wondered if courses could be designed as engineering artifacts were designed. In other words, we wondered if it was possible to apply knowledge of the learning process to the design of a course. We approached this as engineers and began reading the literature in educational psychology and cognitive science. We were particularly interested in work that formed a coherent model of the learning process and techniques that seemed to be based on that sort of model. This book presents our findings, and we indicate where we found different aspects of the model in the literature.

As we have stated already, those who teach should understand how students learn, regardless of the course level or discipline. However, this book applies particularly to teachers of the STEM disciplines. They are more accustomed to thinking in terms of models, so having a model of the process will help in understanding what to do and why something will or might not work.

A Look Ahead

One frequently raised objection is that teachers are doing pretty well despite their lack of knowledge of the learning process. In other words, we seem to manage using common sense approaches in the classroom. However, as Robert Bjork (2002) points out, many of the most effective classroom approaches and important results about how people learn are counterintuitive (p. 3). So, it may take some courage to implement some of the concepts in this book.

In the first chapter, we take some time to provide a rationale for the idea that there really is a problem with what we are doing. We are not surviving as well as we ought to or as well as we may think we are. The first chapter presents evidence that helps us to focus on some problem areas. Despite any good feelings we may have, all is not well, particularly within STEM disciplines.

In the next three chapters we look at a model of the human memory system (Chapter 2), how we perceive material and get it into working memory (Chapter 3), and the evidence that exists for the best ways to process material that is perceived to store that material in long-term memory (Chapter 4). Along the way we will encounter some concepts about just how that material is stored in memory; this will be useful as we consider how to achieve learning that results in long-term retention. In particular, we find strong evidence that active learning techniques very effectively promote long-term retention and improvements in learning.

In Chapter 5 we look at levels of learning interpreted through the lens of Bloom's taxonomy of educational objectives. This categorization gives us a way to classify students' levels of knowing, which are strong determinants of how effective we are in achieving long-term retention. Later in the book we note that various teaching techniques produce learning at different levels and that achieving different levels is important for long-term retention and "transfer."

Chapters 6, 7, and 8 together focus on various topics in active learning. We face a conundrum here because the evidence we encounter in Chapter 4 is not based on a really good definition of active learning. As we proceed through this sequence of chapters—beginning with some commonly advocated methods in Chapter 6 through to a discussion of problem-based learning (PBL) in Chapter 8—we attempt to refine the concept of active learning and regularly refer to concepts from Bloom's taxonomy.

In Chapters 9 and 10 we discuss the multifaceted concept of *transfer*, in which students apply what they learn in different contexts and situations to problems that might not be directly related. STEM teachers know full well that the material students learn today could be outdated in only a few years, so they want their students to be able to adapt to whatever is coming. There is a vast, and rapidly growing, literature on this topic.

Finally, in the last chapter we look at ways the concepts in the book can be used to improve your teaching. This is perhaps the hardest part. Effective techniques, some known for years, never seem to make it into many classrooms. In this final chapter, we address some of the issues that make it difficult for STEM faculty to implement changes.

Maybe you anticipate that some of the techniques you will encounter in this book are chancy—something you find interesting to read about but are wary of using in the classroom. Almost everything presented here has been used successfully by faculty both teaching now and previously. In the 1950s, for example, the engineering curriculum at Carnegie Institute of Technology (as Carnegie-Mellon University was known in those days) implemented many of the ideas in this book. Those faculty had a strong sense of what worked as well as the courage to use what they believed in. They built strong programs using these ideas, and those of us fortunate enough to experience that curriculum realize how powerful their approach was. You can build courses and curricula with that educational and motivational power—and you will have the added advantage of knowing why what you are doing works.

Questions About Teaching and Learning

It makes sense to begin a journey through a book knowing where you are starting. To that end, take several minutes and answer the following questions we assembled by circling your answers. If you think two or more answers could be correct, choose the answer you think is best or the most commonly found result:

1) When a student learns

    a) A copy of what is in the instructor's mind is the goal for what should be in the student's mind after the instruction.

    b) Information is transmitted from the instructor to the student.

    c) Students retain a processed version of the material perceived by the student.

    d) None of the above options are true.

2) Which of these statements are generally true?

    a) Competition pushes students to achieve higher levels of learning than cooperation.

    b) Students master material more effectively if they work independently rather than in groups.

    c) Students must learn the underlying facts, formulae, and theories before being asked to solve real problems.

    d) Lecturing remains the most common instructional method in higher education because it is one of the most efficient methods of delivering information.

3) When students learn a set of material

    a) They either know or don't know the material.

    b) They may be able to explain the material but not be able to apply it.

    c) They may be able to apply the material but not be able to explain it.

    d) None of the above options are true.

4) A clear, logically presented lecture

    a) Leads to deeper understanding than group exercises on the same material.

    b) Allows the instructor to cover more material in the allotted time because students learn faster and better.

    c) Produces learning equivalent to the best active learning methods.

    d) Does not need to be supplemented with hands-on activities.

    e) None of the above options are true.

5) Good teachers

    a) Must have a deep understanding of the material.

    b) Can teach any material.

    c) Have knowledge of the conceptual barriers to learning a particular set of material.

    d) Primarily enhance learning by developing clear and logical lectures.

    e) Improves their lecture when students fail to learn adequately.

    f) None of the above options are true.

6) Learning increases as

    a) Students reread the material.

    b) Lecture time increases.

    c) Activity time increases.

    d) None of the above options are true.

These questions lead to insights regarding how instructors think about the concepts, and answers often reveal some interesting misconceptions about the learning process. In the numerous workshops we have given for faculty in engineering and science, we have posed those questions. A tabulation of attendees' responses (in percentages) is given herein, along with our comments. Note that participants in these workshops may have been predisposed to active learning methods, which could have influenced these results.

Reviewing these results indicates that many instructors (at least those attending our workshops) have fairly good ideas about what are effective pedagogical techniques but that the evidence is not overwhelming. Many of the answers to these questions are fairly widely distributed among the possible answers.

Question	A	B	C	D	E	
1. When a student learns . . .	5	10	70	15		Most picked C, the best answer because learning is a two-stage process.
2. Which statement is true?	12.5	21	21	33		Most picked D, lecturing may deliver information, but students may not retain it.
3. When a student learns . . .	4	25	29	42		D is probably the best, but none of these options is really true.
4. Clear logical lecture	10	0	5	0	85	See the comment on Question 2.
5. Good teachers . . .	26	3	28.5	14	28.5	No, any good teacher cannot teach any material (B). However, clear and logical lectures (D) are not necessarily the best way to go. More on this in later chapters. (And no one picked "None of the above.")
6. Learning increases . . .	24	5	57	14		Increasing activity time (C) may well increase learning, but learning is not necessarily directly related to time on task.

Acknowledgments

This book has been a long journey for us. Many years ago, each of us became interested in education and how to make our courses effective. Along the way we each encountered some extraordinary teachers who inspired and showed us that it was possible—teachers like Dr. Leo A. Finzi and others. Some years ago as we started on this journey we realized that it was going to take a while to assemble the evidence for a clear statement of the learning process, if it was even possible at all. As we proceeded, our wives, Mary Mastascusa, Linda Snyder, and Carolyn Hoyt, provided invaluable support and encouragement, and we thank them for this. In addition, we are deeply indebted to Maryellen Weimer for her advice, support, and faith in the value of this project and without whose help this book never would have come to fruition.

About the Authors

Edward J. Mastascusa, a native of Pittsburgh, Pennsylvania, has three degrees from Carnegie Mellon University. He is a retired professor of electrical engineering at Bucknell University, where he taught for 41 years. His specialty was control systems, and he also taught introductory courses in electrical engineering and instrumentation. He is the recipient of the Bucknell Lindback Award for Distinguished Teaching (1981) and the Distinguished Teaching Award from the Mid-Atlantic Section of the American Society for Engineering Education (1991). Because of his interest in teaching and learning, he has led summer workshops on the subjects for over 10 years.

Professor Mastascusa's experience includes instrumentation design (Magnetics Inc.), control system design (Collins Radio, now part of North American Rockwell, Westinghouse, NASA), and system modeling (NIST). He resides in Lewisburg, Pennsylvania, with Mary, his wife of 50 years.

William J. Snyder left his hometown of Altoona, Pennsylvania, to receive his BS, MS, and PhD degrees in chemical engineering from The Pennsylvania State University. After completing a postdoctoral position at Lehigh University, he joined the chemical engineering department at Bucknell University in 1969 and is still teaching there. He received the Bucknell Lindback Award for Distinguished Teaching and teaches thermodynamics, design, polymers, reaction engineering, and fluid flow. Professor Snyder has been active in developing electronic classrooms, computer-aided laboratories, and has led workshops for faculty on interfacing computers and teaching methods. Dr. Snyder has been a consultant for NASA, NIST, AEC, Mobil Oil, as well as local industry. He is a registered engineer in Pennsylvania and a member of AIChE, ACS, and ASEE.

Dr. Snyder lives in Lewisburg, Pennsylvania, with his wife Linda.

Brian S. Hoyt's quest to better understand the teaching and learning process began as an undergraduate when he began to wonder why he learned in a manner so different from the majority of his classmates. As a result of this growing passion, Brian double majored in electrical engineering and education at Bucknell University. He began his professional career as a high school math and physics teacher. After completing master's degrees in electrical engineering and instructional technology, Brian returned to higher education, working in a variety of capacities focused on applying technology in teaching, learning, communications, and marketing and administrative activities.

Brian currently resides in the Pacific Northwest with his wife, Carolyn, and two sons, Cody and Ian.

1

Is There a Problem?

Or Is the Problem That We Don't Think There Is a Problem?

This chapter examines our educational system to get a clearer picture of its fairly substantial problems. Pinning down exactly what they are is the goal of this chapter.

These observations should make us all think a little:

- "Education is not as effective as it needs to be, should be, and can be, in our nation, particularly math and science" (Bjork, 2004, p. 2).

- "Typical first-year college students . . . are not well prepared for college learning" (Leamnson, 1999, p. 2).

- "Although faculty members want their students to achieve higher kinds of learning, they continue to use a form of teaching that is not effective at promoting such learning" (Fink, 2003, p. 3).

Some of the evidence is anecdotal but still quite convincing and often very entertaining. Late-night television shows and court TV shows illustrate that great entertainment can be found by exposing the ignorance of people. News stories often recount various failings in the educational system. Graduates in some school systems are counted lucky if they can read their own diplomas. Yet evidence to the contrary can be found. An educational system that produces graduates who can't name the current president of the country also produces graduates who can sequence the human genetic code and design integrated circuit chips of ever increasing speed and complexity. This enigma (or is it a dilemma?) needs to be examined to name the problem, if there is one. Let's look for an answer by looking at some of the past research.

Some Evidence for the Problem

Halloun and Hestenes (1985a, in Bain, 2004) did a classic study on how typical introductory physics courses change student conceptions about motion and basic physics concepts related to motion. Going into the course, students carried a lot of baggage often referred to as "Aristotelian physics" and medieval concepts of "impetus." Introductory physics courses are designed to present concepts based on Newton's conception of inertia and the force laws he first propounded. (The students are not expected to cover relativistic concepts, for example.)

What Halloun and Hestenes found is that after the course "even many 'A' students continued to think like Aristotle rather than like Newton . . . They had memorized formulae and learned to plug the right numbers into them, but they did not change their basic conceptions" (Bain, 2004, p. 22). These are disturbing results because they give a clear indication that an introductory physics course did not effectively impart the basic concepts necessary for later courses in physics and any discipline that applies those physical concepts. Halloun and Hestenes then conducted individual interviews designed to probe student understanding further, only to discover that students firmly held on to their misconceptions even in the face of evidence that contradicted those misconceptions. Those students were, however, very adept at devising explanations about why those experiments did not perform as they expected. Unfortunately, Halloun and Hestenes are not alone in concluding that students do not learn what we think they learn in their courses.

Several years ago Philip Sadler (1989), a professor in the education department at Harvard University, began a project that generated a series of very unsettling films. His results on the state of science education confirm what Halloun and Hestenes found. Those results are found in two films.

The Problem of the Seasons

In "Private Theories" (from A *Private Universe*, Sadler, 1989) an interviewer approached recent Harvard graduates (still in their graduation robes) and a few Harvard faculty and asked why it was warmer in the summer than it was in the winter. The commonest answer was that the earth was closest to the sun in the summer, which causes the increase in temperature experienced in the summer.

The correct answer is that the earth's seasons are caused by axial tilt (with respect to the plane of the earth's orbit), so the angle of the sunlight reaching the surface in the northern hemisphere is greatest (closest to verticality) late in June. Interestingly, the earth is closest to the sun in January, when it is coldest in the northern hemisphere—where these students were located. And, if it were a matter of distance, we would have summer at the same time in both North America and South America, and we all know that is not what happens. Finally, it should be noted that clueless students in the film proudly proclaimed that they had taken astrophysics.

Where Does the Wood Come From?

In "Out of Thin Air" (from *Minds of Our Own*, Sadler, 1996), an interviewer asks where the mass in a block of wood comes from. The commonest answer is that wood is composed of material sucked from the earth by tree roots (presumably transmogrified somehow by the tree).

If you burn a piece of wood, the ash that remains is all of the solid material that comes from the earth. The rest is water—some from the roots, some absorbed through the leaves—and carbon dioxide absorbed through the leaves. The bulk of the material in wood is fiber, a carbohydrate composed of carbon and water.

The Lightbulb Problem

In "Batteries and Bulbs" (from *Minds of Our Own*, Sadler, 1996), an interviewer approached very recent Massachusetts Institute of Technology (MIT) graduates, also with robes on, and asked if they could illuminate a lightbulb given three items—the lightbulb, a battery, and a single piece of wire. They were uniformly confident that they could light the bulb, but precious few could actually do it. You can try this experiment with your students if you teach a course that covers basic electrical concepts. It takes very little equipment, and the responses can be revealing. We don't recommend doing it immediately after you have taught an introductory course in electrical engineering to those students.

———————

What happens in these films is very disconcerting because the misconceptions are both fundamental and pervasive. Even after taking courses (in astrophysics) that should have gotten rid of the misconceptions, they persist. If you are interested in the videos, they are available from the Annenberg Foundation, at the URL indicated in the Sadler references.

There are other indications of a problem. You can almost always find a professor who bemoans how poorly prepared students are in his class. Even though he vows that he can do much better, after teaching the prerequisite material he is utterly dismayed that the student are just as poorly prepared. Perhaps you have bemoaned how little your students take from the classroom to apply in the laboratory. And, if you are really curious, you may have talked to students about topics in your class only to find that they have a very shallow knowledge of topics you thought you had taught well.

Either the education we think we are giving to our students is almost totally evanescent, or we never really get through to them in the first place. But have we precisely defined the problem yet? Exam results indicate that students seem to learn material; however, they seem not to retain it, or, when they do, they can't apply it to a real-life problem.

"The Science and Art of Transfer" (Perkins and Salomon, 1990) begins with "a disappointed professor of physics at a nearby college. . . . "

> Among the stock problems explored in the physics course was one like this: "A ball weighing three kilograms is dropped from the top of a hundred meter tower. How many seconds does it take to reach the ground?" [Physics aficionados will recognize that the weight of the ball has nothing to do with the problem; it is a distraction. The answer depends only on the acceleration of gravity.] On the final exam, the professor included a problem like this: "There is a one-hundred meter hole in the ground. A ball weighing three kilograms is rolled off the side into the hole. How long does it take to reach the bottom?" Some students did not recognize the connection between the "tower" problem and the "hole" problem. One student even came up after the exam and accosted the professor with this complaint. "I think that this exam was unfair," the student wailed. "We never had any hole problems!" (p. 1).

Professors of physics or any other sciences and engineering will recognize that there is no conceptual difference between the tower problem and the hole problem. In both problems a ball drops 100 meters, and that is all that counts. Yet many students will find it difficult or will be unable to apply the general knowledge acquired in the tower problem to any other context.

The problem is students' inability to use the material they learn in a course after passing exams and earning a good grade. This material is said to be inert; students cannot transfer it to a new situation. This problem is at the heart of the Sadler–Annenberg films and the anecdote about the hole.

What Do Others Think?

An investigation of the state of education by other individuals and organizations has produced some interesting results. In the first chapter of a report by the National Research Council (NRC) titled *How People Learn* (Bransford et al., 2000), three key findings used to drive material throughout the book are presented:

- "Students come to the classroom with preconceptions about how the world works. If their initial understanding is not engaged, they may fail to grasp the new concepts and information that are taught, or they may learn them for purposes of a test but revert to their preconceptions outside the classroom" (p. 14).

- "To develop competence in an area of inquiry, students must have a deep foundation of factual knowledge; understand facts and ideas in the context of a conceptual framework; [and] organize knowledge in ways that facilitate retrieval and application" (p. 16).

- "A 'metacognitive' approach to instruction can help students learn to take control of their own learning by defining learning goals and monitoring their progress in achieving them" (p. 18).

The first key concept addresses the existence of misconceptions in learners. The essence of this is that misconceptions must be found and addressed, or new learning will simply cover up basic, preexisting misunderstandings and misconceptions. It is hard to argue with that, and the first key finding clearly points to some classroom teaching strategies that seem to make good sense—like identifying preexisting misconceptions.

The second key finding concerns the depth of understanding that students need to achieve. However, this is somewhat fuzzier, with undefined phrases like "deep foundation." Further, a teacher in the classroom will need specific "ways that facilitate retrieval and application." As the old saying goes, the devil is in the details, and many details would be needed to implement this finding.

Finally, there is a call to address metacognitive aspects of learning. The problem with the three key findings is that they all point somehow to things that can be done in the classroom but give us little indication of what is actually taking place inside the students' minds as they learn. Teachers, especially those who teach engineering and science, have a strong tendency to think using an explanatory model. This model is missing from *How People Learn* but would be very helpful when examining recommendations for teaching and learning strategies in the classroom. It would provide a framework to explain why certain classroom strategies work and should be used. In later chapters we present an explanatory model of what takes place as students learn. Details of that model are finding support in various research results.

Many other educators have been concerned with the question of how people learn. An article in *ASEE Prism* (Grose, 2006) cites how a number of universities, including Purdue University, Virginia Tech, and Utah State University, have established not only teaching centers but also departments centered on engineering education. The hope expressed therein is that more are coming. Clearly there is a developing consensus that educators need to understand more about how students learn and how to construct learning situations that maximize what students learn.

Our experience is what motivated us to write this book; we have incorporated into our teaching many of the concepts and ideas we describe herein in our teaching. We are convinced that students learn better—and in some sense more deeply—when these ideas make their way into the classroom. Our students have responded to these approaches with enthusiasm and more focused attention.

As we have become involved with the material in the book we have come to value the research that has been done in this area. However, we have also realized that, though a considerable amount of good work has been done, not everything directly applies to those of us who teach science and engineering content. We have made an attempt to put together work that forms what we think is a coherent whole—a big picture—but that is relevant to our content and teaching contexts. Here's the most important issue and the driving force behind our work in this book: Even the best of us can do better if we learn more about what actually takes place in the minds of the students and if we apply that knowledge in the right way.

Summary

In this chapter we argue that there is a problem in our educational system. Students arrive unprepared for college and bring serious misconceptions with them. College course work does not deal with the misconceptions as directly or effectively as it should. Students leave college unprepared for what awaits them. Moreover, college faculty do not regularly use the teaching methods consistent with research findings. Most are unaware that research in educational psychology and cognitive science has established much about how people learn and the kinds of teaching that promotes that learning.

What's Coming Up

As we proceed, we will encounter numerous recommendations, which we will examine through the lens of a model of the learning process that we develop and present in the next few chapters. Many of the effective methods are counterintuitive. As Bjork (2004, p. 3) observes, "the ways that I see based on basic research to dramatically upgrade instruction, are, in many ways, unintuitive, and counter to prevailing practices."

So, as you proceed through the book, please be prepared to abandon your preconceptions about what might work in the classroom and to entertain some concepts that are "unintuitive, and counter to prevailing practices."

2

Learning and Memory
How Does Learning Happen?

For the teaching–learning process to be effective, it is important to understand what happens in the minds of students trying to learn new material. Every instructor has an implicit model for this, whether or not it can be consciously stated. However, often the model is incorrect because most instructors haven't thought much about what happens in that process. Examining some of the research on the learning process can profoundly impact what we do in the classroom.

Without an accurate understanding of what happens as learning occurs, instructors may not teach effectively. In this chapter we will examine some common misconceptions about and develop a specific model for the learning process. The model uses familiar psychology concepts, which we employ to develop a coherent model of how students learn new material. Instructors can use the model to evaluate teaching strategies and to explain problems when they occur. We start by considering what happens in most classrooms.

What Happens in a Typical Class Period?

Imagine this scenario. You have just attended a class—your first class in transcendental transmogrification (a name chosen because we're pretty sure there is no such course anywhere, and the name shouldn't get in the way of what we have to say). The presenter gave a good lecture assisted by plentiful PowerPoint slides. At the end of the period there was an abbreviated question-and-answer session (because the lecturer just about ran out of time—that's the normal situation, isn't it?), and that was it. You came away thinking you had learned something. But what happened? What will you know about transcendental transmogrification a month later?

Physically, what happened was that the lecturer spoke (i.e., put sound waves into the air) and presented visual material (put light waves into the room). Those sound and light waves conveyed information from the speaker, or the speaker's slides, to you, the learner. This is the physical aspect—the most obvious part—of the experience. Since information is transmitted from the lecturer to the student you may think of this as an information transmission process. But the important part of the learning process is what happens when you receive (perceive) this information and integrate it with the rest of what you know.

After you perceived those signals using physiological mechanisms, you started to process them—the psychological aspect of the lecture. For example, the sequences of phonemes (received as sound waves) were interpreted as words, and you associated those words with previously stored concepts. The same thing happens with visual material. You may perceive lines and spaces of various sorts, but you interpret some of that as textual material and would recognize other material in visual formats. You might not make the right connections. If the speaker said, "The ants are my friends; they're blowin' in the wind," you might hear the words to that old song, "The answer, my friends, is blowin' in the wind." The possibility of misinterpreting visual material also exists, akin to optical illusions where individuals look at the same thing and see different things.

A psychologist would tell you that your interpretation of the information received is quickly passed from the senses (including sensory memory) and is soon stored in your short-term memory (STM). Your short-term memory contains the material your attention is focused during the lecture. And, as the lecture proceeds, the material may move to your long-term memory (LTM). That's where you want it to be at the conclusion of the learning session.

This quick summary of what took place leads us to a couple of important questions: Just exactly when in all of this process did the learning actually take place, and what is important in the process? There is something else buried in this scenario. The model we use to describe what has happened involves some basic concepts from the field of psychology and is very different from the models that lie behind much of what takes place in today's classrooms. Many details in this model need to be explained, the most important of which concern what happens to the information stored in the learner's short-term memory.

Models of the Learning Process

Many implicit models for the learning process justify the use of certain teaching methods (see Bain, 2004 for a discussion of several). For example, many teachers assume that the goal of the learning process is to create a copy in students' minds of what is in the teacher's mind, but there are numerous ways to visualize what might happen as students learn. For example, maybe the teacher tosses the information into students' heads or puts the material into the air, hoping that it passes through students' ears and is eventually copied into their brains. Maybe it pops out of a book as students read and somehow gets into their heads. Those models leave no room for the added processing that "embeds" the new material and links it to what students already know. Learning has more to it than just the reception and storage of information. All the stages of learning—the physical, the perceptual, and the psychological—must be considered.

The idea that learning is simply adding information to whatever else is in students' heads is common. This model goes by several different names, but most versions focus only on the physical stage and do not include the physiological or psychological stages. For example, the banking model, originally described by Freire (1970) and subsequently discussed by many authors such as Bain (2004), compares the student brain to a bank where "deposits of information" are made. The information transmission model, probably a popular term among electrical engineers, is another version of this model, in which information is viewed as being transmitted from the professor's brain to the students' brains— presumably where it is received. These models all share the idea that information can somehow just be put into the mind of the student and that, when this happens, learning is finished. If you lecture for an entire class period, then you are in an information transmission "mode."

At the opposite end of this spectrum are constructivist models of learning. Regarding these models, Stage, Muller, Kinzie, and Simmons (1998) said, "Constructivist approaches emphasize learners' actively constructing their own knowledge rather than passively receiving information transmitted to them from teachers and textbooks" (p. 35). This highlights a number of important points about this approach. First, and most obvious, is that learners construct their own knowledge rather than simply being the recipients of knowledge. Second, they construct actively—and that will eventually take us to active learning. This statement also repudiates the idea of transmission of knowledge.

Constructivist models do not assume that students have to start at the very beginning of every concept and derive everything from first principles. For example, there is no need for students to construct the periodic table on their own. It makes sense to transmit some parts of course content. When we discuss constructing knowledge in students' minds, we mean that all students construct their own knowledge of a particular topic from what is presented and from what they do and think as they interact with that material. All students integrate new material with what is known and, in the process, build a unique knowledge structure in their brain. The structures cannot simply be given to students; they make the material their own. This happens differently among students because they bring different prior knowledge and experience to the learning task and will construct an individual and unique version of the knowledge that is being learned. Instructors can greatly assist students in generating useful knowledge structures by helping them as they work to construct them. In this way the instructor begins to move from a pure transmission mode to a somewhat more constructivist approach. Helping and guiding students to construct knowledge structures is what instruction is really about.

A Historical Note

Research has established that learning is more complex than just the transmission of information from the teacher to the student–learner. What happens to that information, after it is received or perceived by the student, is just as important as getting the information in the first place. Kolb's (1984) work with engineering students at Massachusetts Institute of Technology (MIT) envisioned learning as a process involving two stages: perception and processing. They correspond to the physiological and psychological stages we have already identified, but the terms *perception* and *processing* are preferred and will be used for the rest of the book.

Perception is the act of receiving information through one or more sensory channels and putting that information into short-term memory, identified herein as the physiological stage but could include the physical stage as well. Any perceived information stays for a short time in sensory memory (i.e., memory associated with the particular sense involved) but is quickly passed on to short-term memory. A block diagram representation of the memory model is shown in Figure 2.1.

Processing is the act of integrating perceived information (located in the learner's short-term memory) with information stored in the learner's long-term memory, storing the resultant "melded" information in the learner's long-term memory (i.e., the

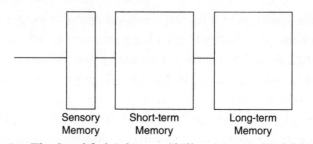

| Sensory | Short-term | Long-term |
| Memory | Memory | Memory |

Figure 2.1 The Simplified Atkinson–Shiffren Memory Model (1968)

psychological stage). Some literature refers to this simply as *integration*. Kolb (1984) indicates that students can perceive in two ways (i.e., actively and passively) and can process in two ways (i.e., actively and passively), giving them four combinations and four different learning styles. Each of those learning styles focuses on a different question: how, why, what, and what if. By helping students discover answers to those questions, an instructor can address the needs of all four learning styles. Harb, Terry, Hurt, and Williamson (2009) refer to this as "teaching through the cycle," but it is more commonly known as the Kolb cycle.

In this two-stage model of perception and processing, when students first receive information it first goes into their short-term memory. The material perceived and stored there is then integrated with what is already known. In that process students construct a personal version of the material—one that is substantively correct but also one that makes sense to them in particular. It is not, and cannot be, an exact copy of the instructor's version because the material is integrated with different prior knowledge and background experiences. In this way students construct knowledge, and we have a constructivist model.

The Process of Constructing Knowledge

The instructor cannot just ask students to take charge of constructing their own knowledge. The process is complex.

You have probably had the experience of asking someone for a telephone number—or some other small piece of information that you had to use almost immediately. Perhaps you got a telephone number and dialed that number immediately. Even though you've done that many times, can you claim that you've "learned" all of those telephone numbers for life? We're guessing you've long forgotten almost every one of those telephone numbers. Some items of information, however, you retain for a long time—measured in days, weeks, months, and often years. Those items, which might include telephone numbers, are things that you have learned.

The difference between things quickly forgotten and things long remembered involves the structure of the memory system in the human brain. Newly perceived information enters the human brain and goes into a system variously called *short-term memory* and *working memory* (Baddeley, 2002, 2007). The two terms are not synonymous, but the differences are not particularly relevant to the points we want to make. (It is possible to view Baddeley's model as a version of short-term memory with more detail.) In either case, "Temporary representations in working memory are subject to rapid decay . . . unless the rememberer is engaged in active maintenance activities" (Gathercole, 2007, p. 156). In other words, if you repeat that phone number over and over you will remember it until you stop repeating it (repeating it is a "maintenance activity"). At that point, it will evaporate and be forgotten.

Among the work done on the structure of working memory, Baddeley's is especially important (see Baddeley, 2007 for a concise summary). His model of the working memory incorporates several items such as the phonological loop (sometimes called a *rehearsal loop*), where the "rememberer" repeats verbal information, and the visuospatial sketchpad, where the rememberer stores things such as pictures and short "videos."

Besides those two components, there is a "central executive" or "executive controller" that supervises and controls interactions between other components of working memory. This important component of working memory distinguishes the concept of working memory from short-term memory. Finally, there is an episodic memory, which serves a number of functions. For example, textual material is perceived in the visual channel but ultimately makes its way to the phonological loop. The real question is what happens after material is perceived and stored in working memory. If nothing is done, then that material—evanescent as it is—will disappear, and no learning will take place. Somehow, the material in working memory has to be stored in long-term memory. If that doesn't happen, then it is not remembered, and not remembered means not learned.

The Overall Model

Several good pictorial models in the literature show the system we have been discussing. Our version in Figure 2.2 is built on them.

This model shows how visual and sound signals make their way through human sensors, through sensory memory, and into working memory. It also shows interactions between signals coming in through the senses and interaction with long-term memory (compare to, e.g., Mayer, 2008, p. 16). Different versions of this model—with slight variations—can be found in numerous references, but the salient features of the model are summarized as follows:

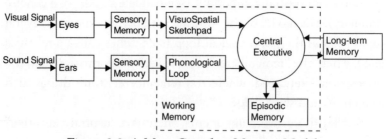

Figure 2.2 A More Complete Memory Model

- Two channels of input—visual and audible—receive sensory input.

- The input signals are stored for a very short time in sensory memory (e.g., you can recall the sound of the last phrase you heard for a very short time).

- Both sets of input signals—the phonological loop and the visuospatial sketchpad—go to short-term memory storage.

- Material can be retrieved from long-term memory as well and brought into short-term memory. Note the arrow going from long-term memory to the central executive.

- Products of processing can also be stored back into long-term memory, as shown by the arrow going from the central executive to long-term memory.

Like any model, Figure 2.2. presents a picture of how the process works. Take it as a pictorial representation of the basic human memory system showing the important interactions within the system. For a good recapitulation see Baddeley (2002) with the cryptic title "Is Working Memory Still Working?"

What Happens to Material in Working Memory?

Getting material from working memory into LTM is called processing the material. If you have ever tried to memorize a poem or a bit of prose, you probably read and reread the material, which enabled you to put it into your long-term memory. But that kind of processing—boring memorization—is pretty inefficient and is not necessarily a good way to learn material if you want to retain it and use it later. In a later chapter we will discuss some active learning methods that are effective for long-term retention and application.

Material can be stored in different ways in LTM. When you memorize material, it makes its way through sensory memory and working (short-term) memory and is stored in the "declarative memory" in the hippocampus (Petty, 2006, p. 11). Anything stored there is usually forgotten within the space of a month or so, so it needs to be processed to be put into a form that can be stored permanently (for a lifetime, possibly) in long-term memory.

If you learn how to use that same material, then it will be stored in a different area of the brain. Thus, the student, by choosing a learning strategy (such as memorization) changes the location and knowledge structure that she constructs in her brain, a possibility instructors should be aware of.

Initially, most material makes its way through sensory memory and working (short-term) memory to be stored in declarative memory. At that point, it is not permanently stored and needs to be processed to be put into a form that can be stored permanently (for a lifetime, possibly) in long-term memory. As Zola-Morgan and Squire (1990) put it: "The hippocampal formation is required for memory storage for only a limited period of time after learning. As time passes, its role in memory diminished, and a more permanent memory gradually develops independently of the hippocampal formation" (p. 288).

So, after being stored in declarative memory (in the hippocampus) what has been "learned" is eventually moved to other, more permanent, locations in the human memory. As Eichenbaum (2004) notes: "The memory processing mediated by the hippocampal system begins during learning and continues to contribute to the consolidation of memories over a prolonged period" (p. 109). That memory processing consolidates memories—putting them into a format suitable for long term storage.

These considerations begin to define what we need to do over the rest of this chapter and the next few chapters. The memory system will be examined in more detail over the remainder of this and the next few chapters. First, we need to discuss working memory's limited capacity and its interactions with long-term memory. Material is stored in long-term memory in a particular way—known as *schemata* in the field of psychology and *knowledge structures* and *engrams* in the field of neuroscience. (Some minor distinctions are made among these concepts, but for our purposes we will consider them the same.) Second, we need to examine the processes by which material is presented and perceived and then processed and stored in long-term memory.

Working Memory Has Limited Capacity

Miller (1956) first wrote that working memory can contain only about seven items, but this is now known to be an urban legend. In a later paper, Chase and Simon (1973), in an interesting study using the game of chess, compared the abilities of novice and expert chess players in remembering positions of chess pieces. The experts were better only when the pieces were arranged as they would have been during a game because the experts remembered combinations (chunks of knowledge). Experts could remember five to nine combinations or chunks, whereas novices could remember only five to nine individual chess pieces.

The idea that working memory can contain seven items, be they simple facts like numbers or larger chunks of information, can be confusing. It's hard to believe that seven items of information take the same amount of memory space regardless of the size of the items. But it may well be that the information itself is not stored in working memory. What's stored there are instead links to the material. (Computer programmers might prefer to think in terms of pointers.)

The storing of chunks of information applies to more than just the visual representations of chess pieces, as in the Chase and Simon (1973) study. How the information is chunked can confound both novices (like beginning students) and experts (like college teachers). In the old days when telegraphers had to learn

Morse code, they started by learning individual letters as a sequence of longs and shorts. In time, they recognized words; true experts would remember entire phrases. Likewise, students in biology might not think in terms of all the members of a particular genus when thinking of characteristics of a life-form, for example. But the biology instructor might think in those terms, chunking together all of the oaks, for example. Or students might have difficulty understanding statements that apply to something like an entire digestive tract if they are just learning all of the components of that biological system. As the old saying goes, some folks cannot see the forest for the trees. The expert (teacher) sees the forest and has to be wary when the novice (student) is looking at single trees. The progression from novice to expert in many disciplines is mostly about finally being able to see the larger picture—the chunks that the experts see automatically.

This progression from novice to expert raises several interesting questions. Exactly what is the difference in the organization of the memory of a novice and an expert? If we can understand that, we can better help our students become experts. And we still haven't explained how chunks of information take the same space in memory as single items of information. How can working memory hold seven chunks when chunks surely have a highly variable size?

What Is Long-Term Memory?

Knowledge Structures, Schemata, and Engrams

To be accessed, material in long-term memory has to have some sort of organization. It has to be stored in a way that allows you to retrieve information that is related. Imagine looking at a piece of paper. The piece of paper in your mind is a representation of the actual piece of paper. Even when you think you "see" a piece of actual paper, your mind is experiencing a representation of that piece of paper—not the real piece of paper. The paper is in your hands, but the image of the paper that you see in your mind is a set of electronic signals in your nerve cells.

The internal representation in your brain is important. Dudai (2007, p. 14) says, "We can, and we should, think about memory as knowledge encoded in brains." That knowledge is encoded in the electronic circuitry of the neurons in the brain—or as Dudai (p. 15) describes it, "a neuronally encoded structured version of the world." At this point, there may not be enough known about exactly how a picture of a piece of paper is encoded in the brain, but it is clear that the representation is stored in large and highly organized neuronal circuitry.

Let's once again imagine that you're memorizing something to be stored in long-term memory. Chances are good it's been stored there sequentially. If you ever tried to start reciting a poem somewhere in the middle, you probably found it difficult. It's much easier if you start reciting from the first line because each part of the poem is linked to the next piece sequentially. The knowledge representation that you built in the process of memorizing your material was a linear structure stored in long-term memory.

However, there is more to memory than just facts linked together in linear structures. Ultimately, your mind stores related material together. For example, in the Chase and Simon (1973) study, chess experts stored patterns of pieces. They had to remember the different pieces, but they also stored how those pieces appeared on the board—their spatial relationships, those chunks we discussed previously. We need to understand that mode of storage in more depth. The next section examines this concept, discusses some vocabulary relevant to memory storage, and develops an analogy that will help us to understand some of the salient facts.

How Is Material Stored in Long-Term Memory?

Learned material is stored in schemata in long-term memory. In the last section we just assumed (as many researchers have) that we could talk in terms of chunks. However, material is stored in more complex structures than just chunks and the concept of schemata is a useful way of thinking about that knowledge organization. Researchers describe how the knowledge is organized in a variety of different ways. We're going to keep it simple and use schema (or schemata, if there's more than one) and knowledge structures when we refer to this concept.

Schemata hold more than just a list of facts about a topic and have been categorized in several basic ways. A schema could contain information about a subject, often arranged as a list of facts related to a subject; we encountered an example of a linear schema when we discussed memorizing a poem. A schema could also contain a visualization (a picture or a graphical representation) of information pertinent to the subject. Or a schema could contain a set of rules or procedures to be used in specific situations. Often those rules, or procedures, refer to ways to use other information in the schema. For example, a schema for interest rates might include a rule for calculating the effective yearly rate of interest paid given the simple yearly interest and the periods when the interest is paid (e.g., quarterly).

Using another illustration, a schema for a restaurant might include the facts you have stored for a typical restaurant, including tables, chairs, menus, and a cash register. It would also include anything that you normally associate with a restaurant, like things you do in a restaurant. You enter the restaurant and choose or are assigned a table. You decide what you want based on the menu and then give your choice to a waiter. Once your food arrives, you eat it. You pay your bill, leave a tip, and exit the restaurant.

The schema for a restaurant will probably include both of these kinds of information: the list of restaurant facts (i.e., declarative knowledge); and the scripts for what you normally do in a restaurant (i.e., procedural knowledge). In addition to containing declarative and procedural knowledge, your schema for a restaurant might also have links to other, related, schema. For example, restaurants always have restrooms, and you have schemata for them. Restaurant bills can be paid with credit cards, and you have a schema for the facts and procedures you need to know to pay a bill with a credit card.

To summarize, a schema can contain at least these items:

- General verbal information (e.g., when memorizing the Gettysburg address)

- Sequential material (lists)

- Pictorial or graphical information

- Scripts (a sequence of steps to accomplish something—a procedure)

- Links to related schemata

We've used a simplified version of schemata to introduce you to the concept. With a complex schema, a person can draw inferences about the subject material. For example, a schema for a bank checking account would include knowledge about checks, deposits, and balances as well as scripts about how to write a check and how to balance the checkbook. It would also probably include links to things like banks in general and savings accounts. However, a person with a good schema would be able to infer that there would be trouble if he attempted to write an check for more than was in the checking account and that he would not be able to use his money from a third-party check immediately after having deposited it. As another example, a schema in geometry for a right triangle would include knowledge about triangles, scripts for calculating the length of the third side given the length of the other two sides, and links to information about other kinds of triangles. But students should also be able to infer that a right triangle cannot have one of the other angles greater than 90 degrees.

What Happens as Students Learn?

Whenever students learn, in terms of schemata at least one of two things can happen to the new material. Either an entirely new schema can be constructed in the mind of the learner that could conceivably incorporate material from other existing schemata, or an existing schema can be modified with the new material being assimilated into the existing schema. In the second scenario, it is possible that the modified schema could be stored separately from the preexisting schema, which effectively serves as a template.

As we begin to think about processing material this mental model will come in handy and will provide us a way of understanding what is happening. We will also need a better understanding of schemata, their organization, and how schemata are created and modified as learning takes place. Let's start with an analogy between schemata and something familiar.

An Analogy Between Schemata and Web Pages

The actual mental model can be compared to a Web page, which comes in many different forms and contains the following:

- Information, often in the form of lists. Even the simplest Web page can be thought of as a list of words. The Web page also often contains pictorial information in addition to the textual kind of material.

- Scripts that examine what you do and then take certain predetermined actions, including selecting books from a book-selling Web site. You enter information like the ISBN, you click an icon when you are ready to purchase, and the Web site takes some action, such as calculating the charge for what you picked.

- Links to other Web pages, either on that particular Web site or to pages anywhere in the electronic universe.

Now, consider some of the attributes and actions for a Web page and compare that to those of schemata. To take the analogy a bit further we have also indicated some analogous properties of computer memory and human memory:

	Web Pages	Schemata
Loading	Loaded from a server. Information on a hard drive describing the page is stored in random access memory (RAM) on the user's computer.	Brings a schema (or links to the schema) from long-term memory into short-term memory, and you activate that schema.
Lists	Contain lists of words, or bulleted lists	Contain a list of things or properties, like the objects found in a restaurant in the restaurant schema
Scripts	Perform according to a set of rules like when calculations are performed or JavaScript describes the actions to be taken.	Schemata identify a sequence of actions to be taken in a particular situation, like the list of actions taken in a restaurant
Links	Link to other Web pages and let the user load the referenced Web page	Link to other schemata and let the learner activate the referenced schema. Unlike Web pages, only schema within the mind of the learner can be accessed.
Short-term Memory	Loaded from RAM (i.e., dynamic memory component of a computer)	Use short-term memory (or, closely equivalent, working memory)

(*Continued*)

	Web Pages	Schemata
Long-term Memory	Use programs that have been installed and stored on the hard drive. Material on the hard drive is not normally used until it is loaded into the RAM.	Contain the total of the person's experience. Material here can be loaded into short-term memory and then acted upon.

The many similarities between Web pages and human memory make this analogy very useful. Of course, it's not a perfect analogy. For example, you can download schemata stored only in your mind (analogous to loading a file from your own computer), but you can't download a schema from someone in Australia even though you can download a Web site from a server in Australia. Still, the analogy can serve as a good way of thinking about what is happening. And the Web page analogy contains the critical features that help us understand what takes place as a learner learns—the sequential (list) information, the presence of scripts, and the existence of links to other similar items in memory.

The Importance of Connections

As we proceed we need to keep in mind that the interconnections or links between schemata are very important in the learning process. Writers often comment on linkages and connections— particularly noting the importance of those connections, especially when the learner later wants to use the material being learned. Patti Shank (2004) in the *eLearners Development Journal*, notes that "People often do not understand how what they know can be applied in various situations because they often don't make the connections we expect them to make" (p. 2). Perkins and Salomon (1994) note, "People often do not understand how what they know can be applied in various situations" (p. 64). So the richness of interconnections between schemata is important in using them as well as what you have learned.

Perception, Processing, and Schemata

New material that has been perceived will ultimately be stored in one or more schemata. That might be a completely new schema or one of the schemata that the learner already possesses, or schemata that the learner possesses might be activated as the learner perceives the new material. The point is that the concept of a schema provides us with a model of what can and should be stored during the processing stage as schemata are constructed. As we investigate the schemata of experts in a field we begin to get a clearer idea of what we should be aiming for in the students. Although we might think that the material will be perceived similarly by most students, some differences in perception and processing need to be considered. Despite these differences, however, the ultimate goal is pretty much the same: We want all of our students to become experts.

Expert Schemata

It is known that the schemata of experts in a given field are more complex and richer (more sophisticated) than those of nonexperts.

> The sophistication of a knowledge structure is defined in terms of its complexity, its level of integration (interconnectedness) and its structural closeness to the experts' knowledge. Complexity and integration are the main characteristics that differentiate the knowledge structure of the expert from that of the novice. More able individuals have richer, more interconnected knowledge structures than do less able individuals. As expertise is attained through learning, the elements of knowledge become increasingly interconnected. In addition to growing more complex and better integrated, the semantic networks of novices also become more structurally similar to those of an expert with learning.

> It is not just the number of elements of knowledge (complexity) and the number of connections between these elements (integration) that matter, but also which particular connections are made (structure). (Khalifa and Shen, 2006, p. 154)

At the conclusion of the learning process the student's schemata should resemble the expert's schemata. We should be aiming for complex and highly interconnected schemata, but to do this we need to know their essential characteristics (abstracted from the quote above):

- Expert schemata have a complex knowledge structure, and those schemata are integrated.

- Expert schemata are richer and more interconnected.

- The particular connections and links in expert schemata are an important part of what makes the person an expert. In other words, an expert in a field will have particular connections to related material, and even though another person has a rich schema, without those particular connections the person will likely perform at a novice level.

We suspect that many of these links are of an "experience" nature. For example, a hurricane expert would be able to bring to mind quickly characteristics of the horrendous hurricane early in the 1900s that hit Galveston, Texas, as well as the surprising hurricane that struck the east coast of New England in September 1938. People don't really become experts until they acquire those particular links. They could be described as part of the culture of experts in a particular field. It behooves us to think about the implications of schemata in a learning context, particularly in the context of what normally happens in a classroom. The characteristics and features of schemata have a strong influence on how we learn, and we need to concern ourselves with how schemata are generated and stored. The next section considers what kind of schemata result in a typical learning situation and what a new schema might be like.

Building Schemata

What Might a New Schema Be Like?

Imagine a student who has just attended a 15-minute electronic slide presentation. What will be stored in the student's mind as she walks out of the room? Remember, whatever is stored, it will be a schema, a knowledge structure, of some sort. But what are the details? Several things could be remembered, but whatever ends up in the student's long-term memory will be made from what is in her short-term memory when the schema is constructed. Various information can be stored in the student's short-term memory.

- The student could retain the text or verbal information that was on the slides.

- The student could retain an image of what was on the slides that could be visualized subsequently.

- The student could retain both the text and the slide images.

- The student could retain an image of the room (e.g., views out the window, color of the wall) in which the presentation occurred.

- The student could retain memories of what the instructor wore that day.

- The student could retain memories of an annoying construction sound caused by work just outside the classroom.

All of these items could be packaged in a knowledge structure (i.e., a schema) in the student's mind as soon as the presentation is over. Several things about this process are not good. Some of what is packaged with the material is totally irrelevant to the topic. The entire schema could well be totally disconnected from anything else that the student knows.

As bad as this might sound, this kind of schema is produced in many classroom situations and may include other contextual elements. "These additional context factors include the learner's prior knowledge, the learner's expectations about the purpose of the original learning, the teacher's expectations of the learner, the learner's internal states during learning and transfer, group versus individual learning in relation to group versus individual application of knowledge, as well as the physical environments of the learning and transfer situations" (Mestre, 2002, p. 9).

We don't often consider the "physical environments of the learning and transfer situations" to be important except for the physical comfort of the learner. But it is possible that elements of the physical environment can be connected with the material to be learned. In this case the instructor has to be prepared to help students remove extraneous items from the schemata in their minds. The original schemata they produce will need to be processed into schemata that are more usable so that they will be able to access that material later without being cued by being in the same room where the material was learned originally.

This phenomenon is called "place learning" (Haskell, 2001). Haskell notes, "Sometimes what is learned is welded to the place where it is learned, because the physical place provides the cues necessary for retrieving the learning" (p. 29). Haskell also points out that we have all had the experience of not being able to recognize someone when we encounter them in surroundings other than where we normally see them. We also can't retrieve something we know when the surroundings don't give the retrieval cues. One of us gave a short quiz using lab data, and the students did well on the quiz in the classroom. But when the students went to the lab (different physical surroundings) and took data themselves, they were unable to do well even though the lab data were virtually the same as the data they used in the classroom.

Other Possible Connections

If the material is something that connects to something previously learned so that the schema being built is not entirely new, then the new schema could also contain any number of misconceptions. For example, children can merge the concept of a round Earth into a previously held schema of a flat Earth (Vosniadou and Brewer, 1992) by modifying their original schema into one in which the earth is pancake shaped. The possibilities for the new schema are as follows:

- The net result is that the initial schemata formed by students after new material is learned could be one of two possibilities.

    - Children could use the material to build a new schema, which will probably contain several different kinds of information.

    - Children could use the material to modify an existing schema, creating a new schema from the new material and what they already know (the preexisting schemata).

- The new schema can contain the textual material presented by the instructor.

- The new schema can contain visual material presented.

- The new schema can contain irrelevant material from the context—particularly the physical surroundings during learning.

- The new schema may well not contain any links to previously known material; it could be added to the children's previous schema.

- That previous schema could contain misconceptions that the new knowledge is added to, producing a larger set of misconceptions.

When you consider the possibilities, it does not seem promising. But the job of the instructor at this point is to take what there is and help the student to build and modify schemata so that the knowledge can be accessed and used wherever and whenever the student needs to do that. We start by examining what often (typically?) takes place in the classroom so that we can clarify still further what those initial schemata might be like.

An Example

We will use an example from physics: teaching Kirchhoff's Current Law (KCL), which can be stated simply as "The sum of the currents entering a node equals zero." If this is memorized, it could be entered into memory as three consecutive short phrases as shown in Figure 2.3.

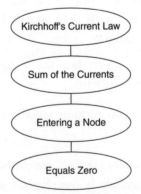

Figure 2.3 Simple Expression of Kirchhoff's Current Law

When students initially encounter the concept of Kirchhoff's Current Law, it is usually expressed as a simple sentence. However, the concept is much more complex, and as time goes on, if students work to enrich their personal representation of KCL, they might develop a more complex knowledge structure—one that is not linear (Figure 2.4).

As students continue to learn, the knowledge structure would probably become more complex and would have links to other knowledge structures students already have (e.g., water flow in a pipe, ways to do summations).

What Is the Present State?

In many science, math, and engineering classrooms, material is still presented by lecture (Fink, 2003), many of which are accompanied by PowerPoint slides or material on transparencies. Most or all of the time is given to presenting material. There may be some inter-action, but many instructors prefer to finish the presentation before entertaining questions, which regularly means little or no time for questions.

At the end of the lecture, instructors often assign problems from the relevant chapter in the textbook, which later, alone or

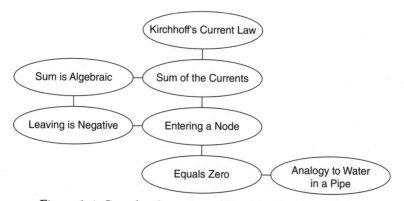

Figure 2.4 Complex Structure of Kirchhoff's Current Law

in a group, they work on. By doing that, we leave the processing to the students. There are several things to note about this kind of approach. First, the time in class is principally devoted to presentation so that students are at the perception stage of the learning process during class time. Little time in class is given to processing the information. At the end of class, students flush their short-term memory and leave the classroom, going on to something else, probably in another course, where completely different material will be covered. The implication of this is that students most probably leave with a schema for the material that is little more than a list of the main points covered in the presentation. Linear schemata (i.e., simple declarative knowledge) are not what we should be aiming for. They do not have the interconnectivity that expert schemata usually possess.

Second, if the instructor assigns some textbook problems to be worked, then the time spent working textbook exercises is where processing is done. When the students begin to work the assigned textbook problems, they first retrieve the material from their long-term memories. Since they did not process that material in class, they need to depend upon their memory to retrieve facts stored with few, if any, connections to related material—a very simple schema, probably with no scripts or links, just pure declarative knowledge. Often they will use their class notes or the text chapter to help them remember. This processing is done without much input from the instructor and depends on students' decisions. In cases where the instructor assigns readings (and no problems), then the processing will probably take place when the student studies for a quiz or exam.

This situation inverts the two stages of the learning process. As we will discover when we examine the processing stage, deep learning takes place when learners construct those links to other material that they know. This means that processing should occupy much more time in the classroom. It also means that reading the chapter or viewing an online presentation should be done before students come to the class. Then the instructor can briefly review the material to help students retrieve the material from short-term memory. This permits the instructor to give more time to the processing stage during class time. When that happens, the instructor can guide the processing as it occurs helping students to a deeper understanding of the material.

Visualizing Schemata Using Concept Maps

The concept of schemata as mental structures that contain representations of knowledge is powerful. Obtaining information about students' various schemata is valuable and useful in helping instructors to guide their learning.

But Who Has Ever Seen an Electron—and Who Has Ever Seen a Schema?

People who work in electronics have never seen an electron, and they never will. Likewise, schemata are knowledge constructs that exist solely within the brain and, in their most elemental form, consist of groups of human neurons wired together in some presently unknown way. So there is a real question as to whether they could ever be seen. In that way they are like electrons.

Unlike electrons, however, there may be a way to get a visible representation of a schema by having the learner draw something called a "concept map." This can be used to graphically represent the concepts and interrelations that exist within schemata and would show the essence of a schema. The best way to understand how a concept map works is to create one.

Drawing a Concept Map

To draw a concept map, follow these instructions:

- Get a clean sheet of plain, unlined paper.

- Close all your notes, and do this from memory.

- Choose something from your discipline that you know well:

  - A geologist might choose continental drift.

  - A chemist might choose a "family" in the periodic table.

  - An electrical engineer might choose "amplifiers."

  - A physicist might choose conservation of energy.

Start by writing down the main concept that you want your concept map to address. Write it in the center of the page, and draw a circle or ellipse around it. (Some advise printing in capital letters; the rationale is that using capital letters forces you to keep it short.)

- Write down one or more related concepts. Draw lines from your main concept to the related concepts.

- Items that are strongly related could have heavier connecting lines.

- Keep drawing more concepts. Now you can include concepts that are related to the second ones you drew. You can think of these as secondary and tertiary concepts or as subconcepts.

- Don't try to impose an organization on what you do. Just let it flow from your mind to the paper. Think of it as a "brain dump."

- You can incorporate color for things related to different subconcepts, or you can draw larger circles around concepts that seem to form natural groupings.

- Remember, concept maps don't have fixed formats, although they are generally not linear structures. Don't try to impose a format on what comes out. Just let it flow.

- The nonlinear structure of the map is natural. It is probably a good representation of the way you have things organized in your mind.

- The nonlinear structure of the map lets you add new items in any direction, and you shouldn't have to erase to fit things in.

What Does This Process Yield?

When you are done, you have a picture that is a group of nodes connected by links: a classical graph, as defined by many mathematicians. Yet this concept map is a strange creature and has been seen in many different incarnations. *Writing the Natural Way* (Lusser-Rico, 1983) describes a technique called clustering that is designed to help writers. The instructions for clustering are almost identical to the instructions for generating a concept map. Although these clusters are intended to help writers, it seems clear that the technique helps writers see what they have within them as they begin to write.

The area of graph theory within mathematics also works with structures—composed of nodes and branches. Graph theory has been applied extensively in many areas of science and engineering, and there are many mathematical techniques developed to extract properties of those graphs. As an example of a pertinent mathematical technique, Turns, Atman, and Adams (2000) compared student concept maps and concept maps generated by experts in an area and found that "concept map construction can be a viable alternative to a traditional final exam" (p. 168).

A Point of Difference

It seems clear that concept maps can give a snapshot of a schema that a person possesses for a particular topic. But the snapshot is incomplete. Although the concept map shows concepts and their relationships, it does not show procedures. To illustrate this

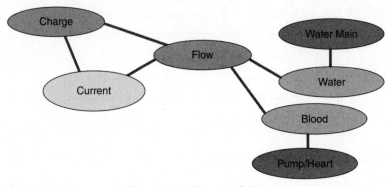

Figure 2.5 Concept Map

point, consider the concept map for the concept flow, shown in Figure 2.5.

In this map, the student has related the concept of flow to blood, water, and electrical charge. However, there are formulas that allow you to calculate flow rate for some of these quantities, and those formulas (procedures!) should be included in the concept map if it is to be a good representation of the schema for flow.

How Can You Use Concept Maps?

Concept maps give the instructor one way to get some insight about the schemata that a student brings to a course. By asking students to draw concept maps for prerequisite material, for example, the instructor can see how complex and well linked this material is in the minds of the students. And since some literature suggests that students have a better understanding of material when their concept maps match the concept maps of experts in the field, the instructor could make a concept map of his or her own and compare that with those of the students in the course.

Figure 2.6 presents an example of a concept map produced by a student entering a course in chemical reaction engineering. This concept map was drawn by the student after being given the set of instructions provided earlier in the chapter.

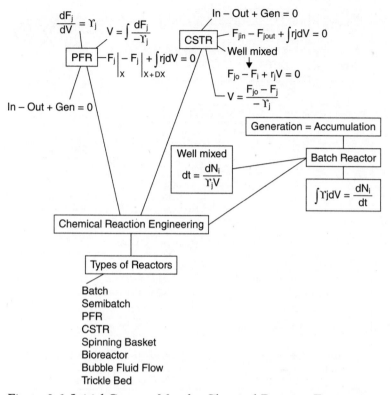

Figure 2.6 Initial Concept Map for Chemical Reaction Engineering

Figure 2.7 shows a concept map from the same student after the course.

It seems evident that a change has take place in the schema of the student as you view the two concept maps. It may or may not be the amount or type of change you wanted, but an instructor can get a lot of information from the comparison. We will discuss aspects of this later.

Summary

To review, the constructivist model of learning, as opposed to various transmission models, is a good model of the learning

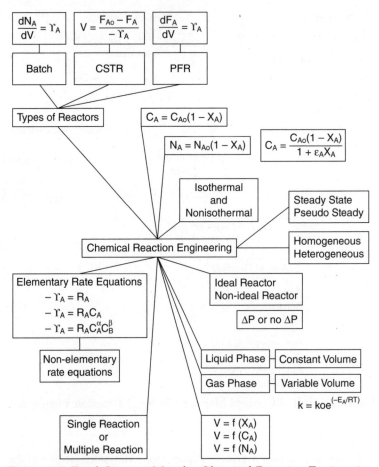

Figure 2.7 Final Concept Map for Chemical Reaction Engineering

process. To teach effectively, you need to understand the memory system in the human mind. This includes knowledge of how material is perceived, particularly the two-channel verbal and visual model. In addition, it is necessary to understand the structure of working memory, including the rehearsal loop; the visuospatial sketchpad, the central executive, and the episodic memory. The chapter reviewed how material is stored in long-term memory and discussed concepts of schemata and what they might contain (e.g., list, pictures, links) as well as how schemata are analogous to a

Web page and the importance of connections within schemata. Place learning is a part of this process. In addition, the chapter covered concept maps as a way of visualizing a schema, including clustering, point of difference, and how the maps be used in instruction.

What's Coming Up

So far we have looked at an overall description of the system. What we haven't done is examine how the system works. Instructors need to understand not just the structure of the system but also how to get the system producing the kind of learning that is desired.

There are two important stages in the learning process when viewed with the memory system in mind. The first stage is getting material into short-term memory. Students need to perceive material and get it into short-term memory taking memory limitations into account, and we will take up that issue in the next chapter. However, learning really occurs only when material is stored in one or more schemata in long-term memory. Only then can the material be retained and accessed when needed at a later time. The learner needs to process material in short-term memory so that it can be stored in long-term memory in a form that is more permanent and accessible. We take that topic up in Chapter 4.

There is some evidence (see Reiner et al., 2001) that students arrive with primitive (naïve) schemata for fundamental physics concepts and that many schemata are not constructed from scratch but rather are modified schemata based upon preexisting naïve schemata, which are then saved in a new format much like a prototype file can be edited and saved under a new name. However, Reiner and coauthors do suggest that features of the prototype schema are hard to eliminate. Their paper is well worth reading and food for thought.

3

Perception

When All Else Fails, Start at the Beginning

In the last chapter, we explored how learning has two stages—perception and processing. In this chapter we will examine some details of perception and some specific instructional strategies during this stage. We are assuming instructors are interested in presenting material in ways that that enhance students' ability to learn the material.

As students perceive material and position it in their short-term memory, the single most important fact is where the students are at the end of that process. We need to know the answers to questions like these:

- What material is actually in short-term memory after the material has been presented?

- What connection does that material have to what students already have stored in long-term memory?

- What can be done at this point to embed the material in students' long-term memory? This question really concerns the schema that students are constructing. What form will that schema take? Will it be an abstract form?

As we present material, we are getting students ready for the processing stage. Some instructors miss that point and assume that once they have presented the material that's it for the learning process—or at least the instructor's part in the learning process. When you arrive in class and lecture the entire time, taking only a few questions, students process very little of the information you are presenting. That approach to teaching is based on an implicit assumption that presentation of the material is the totality of the learning process and that the net result of the learning process is that a copy of the material in your mind ends up in students' minds.

Clearly, some of the material presented will make its way into long-term memory and be remembered, but there is substantial evidence that not much of that material is retained and that much of what is retained is not in the most usable form (see, e.g., Haskell, 2001, Chapter 1; Roediger and Karpicke, 2006). To improve retention and make the material useable, some processing of the material is required. We'll deal with that issue in the next chapter.

We are assuming that you have some ideas on how you want the students to encounter that material initially. For example, you might simply want to present the material in a lecture format. However, you could also plan to have the students encounter a problem in the laboratory and then discuss it further in class. The point is that instructors need to focus on what they want to achieve with the presentation and where the students should be at the conclusion of the presentation.

What Do We Want Students to Get from the Perception Stage?

Assume that you're going to present the material and that your goal is for students to have this material resident in their short-term memory at the end of the presentation. As we discuss how to achieve that goal, we will use the model presented in the previous chapter as a tool to evaluate what should and should not be happening during this stage of the learning process.

The model presented in Chapter 2 for the process of perception is relatively simple and involves a learner getting sensory input in short-term memory, either in the visual–spatial sketchpad or in the rehearsal–phonological loop. This model is straightforward but is a bit oversimplified. There are several caveats worth noting. First of all, not everything that is presented makes its way into short-term memory. If you are sitting in an audiovisual presentation, there could be many distractions. The model we have been using is not a passive system. Learners can take control of what is passed from the sensory input channels into the short-term memory. What students pay attention to is determined by a number of variables.

An Example of Selective Perception

One of us passed around some sensors for students to examine. The sensors could be partially disassembled to see what was inside. Some students (most, in fact) did not have enough curiosity to disassemble them until the instructor explicitly pointed out that the sensors could be taken apart. You need to encourage curiosity to help students maximize their sensory perceptions. In this case, students were perfectly willing to forego a chance to perceive some things that were easily possible to perceive.

The lesson here is that students can and will perceive what they want to perceive. Perception is, at best, only partially under the control of the person presenting the information. Yes, even perception takes a conscious desire on the part of the learner if material is to be accurately and completely perceived.

Whatever happens, we need to be cognizant that there can be many interruptions and that we want to control, as much as possible, the material in students' short-term memories, even if we have to direct their attention to what we want them to observe and perceive.

The Presentation

In your presentation you might want to bring several points together for students to draw a conclusion or to see the connections between several aspects of the material. Your goal is to present those points in a way that leaves the students with those points in their short-term memory. In this section we will consider some simple suggestions to improve that process.

Short-Term Memory Is Limited

Short-term memory can contain only about seven items. The obvious implication is that you can overload the short-term memory by asking students to hold more information there than is possible (Baddeley, 2002, 2007; Mayer, 2003; Miller, 1956). If you need to put together 17 points to draw a conclusion, then your first task is to see how you can subdivide the material to draw the conclusion in stages. Students should not be expected to consider all 17 points concurrently.

Be Careful About What You Present to Students

We do not recommend using motivational stories, even though some would disagree with us. If you are making a sequence of points that you want the students to work with and the third point has a good motivational story associated with it, then when you tell that story the students may well flush all of the preceding material from their short-term memories and remember only the story. Remember, short-term memory capacity is limited and your motivational story could displace material that you wanted to stay in short-term memory. We think (and some experts agree with us; see, e.g., Mayer, 2003) that motivational material is better positioned early in your presentation before you begin discussing the points that you want students to focus on. As a general rule, once you start on your main points, stick to the subject, keep going, and don't introduce anything extraneous.

There are times when you may introduce extraneous material inadvertently. For example, you could have finished a portion of a presentation and be discussing something else, but if you leave a slide up with textual material while you verbally introduce something else, the textual material on your slide might interfere with what you are talking about, thereby overloading the students' short-term memory capacity for verbal material (i.e., the rehearsal loop). Consider inserting a blank slide between every slide with text so you can move on and have discussion but without new or old material showing and possibly distracting students.

What Happens to the Material in Short-Term Memory? What Do We Want to Happen?

There are several options for what can happen to material in the short-term memory. The ultimate goal is for the material in short-term memory to end up in long-term memory, where it should be embedded in schemata (either in newly constructed schemata or in existing schemata), enriching what students already know.

First, material in working memory can stay there as other material is added or deleted. But the short-term memory can become overloaded, and some material may be inadvertently flushed from the short-term memory. Second, material in short-term memory can be moved to long-term memory. In other words, it gets remembered and learned.

Material can be stored in long-term memory in several different ways. We can think of storage in long-term memory in terms of an analogy with file folders. The material can be stored in a new file folder and reside there with no connection to any other material. That would correspond to construction of a completely new schema. Another option is that the material can be stored in a new file folder along with other, related, material in the short-term memory and long-term memory. That would correspond to embedding or linking the newly perceived material to a preexisting schema. Or the material can be stored in a file folder that contains unrelated information. More likely, the newly perceived material could be stored in places where the material is related in ways that we do not expect. For example, the material could be copied into a number of different, but related, file folders. Or notes could be put into related file folders that point to where the new material is located. Finally, material in short-term memory can just be forgotten, not flushed out from overload but simply moved to the mental trash bin. These observations have several implications for teachers.

Don't fill up a period with lecture. If you lecture the entire period, you overload the short-term memory and leave no time for processing. At the end of the period the students will flush the material from their short-term memories with the barest minimum of processing.

When you think that students' short-term memories are getting full, stop presenting material and start to process what you have presented. We will talk about how to process material in the next chapter. Be careful with complex material. Sweller and Chandler (1994) make the claim that some material is simply so complex that cognitive overload (overloading short-term memory) is impossible to avoid without a restructuring of the material. You should always leave time for processing at the end of a period. It's not the time but the total number of items you leave unprocessed in short-term memory. And don't interrupt the "flow" until you are ready to start processing.

If you have presented material and it is in students' short-term memory, do something to help them process the material. That could be a short collaborative exercise, for example. What you shouldn't do is something completely different that requires the students to flush the new material out of their short-term memories. Instead, you should go to some other kind of activity that works with the newly presented material, helping students to store the material in a more usable form in long-term memory, relating or linking that material to something already known.

Adding interesting but irrelevant material to a presentation detracts from effective learning. The irrelevant material may well displace something relevant (Mayer, 2003). If you have just lectured on material, move immediately to something that helps students to process that material. This is not a good time for motivational material (i.e., "Why do you want to learn this material?" Get that out of the way before you start lecturing.). When material is fresh in students' minds, work with that material. Don't ask them to store it temporarily in long-term memory only to retrieve it later for processing.

Don't obsess about content. If you follow these suggestions you will probably find that you are going to cover less. However, the upside to less content is that students learn what you do cover at a deeper level, and there is a better chance of long-term retention. There is way too much material in most courses, and covering all of the material typically results in students memorizing some material for the short term but leaving the course without retaining as much as you want. Less can be more.

Check what students have actually perceived. A good presentation does not ensure correct perception by the learner. Many different things can and will go wrong. This may be the time to give a short exercise requiring students to explain what has been presented. As they do this, they are also making connections to their knowledge store, and this can be the beginning of processing.

Some Further Points

Clark and Mayer (2003) address some interesting questions about presenting with both verbal and pictorial information. In regard to whether it is better to show pictorial material before, after, or simultaneous with the verbal material, Mayer's (2003, p. 64) references indicate that "simultaneous presentation results in deeper learning than successive presentation, as shown by eight studies in which students viewed a narrated animation about lightning, brakes, pumps or lungs." Mayer refers to this as the "Contiguity Principle." As to whether it is better to have just text, just pictures, or a combination of both, Clark and Mayer (2003, pp. 51–65) indicate that using both media helps build connections for the learner and help the process of integration. They refer to this as the "Multimedia Principle." As to whether it is better to have spoken words and an animation or text with the animation, again Clark and Mayer (pp. 83–95) indicate that it is better to have spoken words. Apparently, visual text interferes with perception of a visual animation, and it is better to have the verbal material perceived audibly. They refer to this as the "Modality Principle." Don't add redundant text to a simulation if you have a voice-over or if you plan to explain the simulation. And, clearly, you don't want to read electronic slides during the entire presentation.

Clark and Mayer (2003) offer some other general helpful remarks. They recommend using a conversational, first-person style when presenting verbal material. When possible, let the learners control the rate of presentation, which is easiest when using Web-based presentations. Finally, they recommend using signals (like enumeration) that alert learners to the main points.

Clark and Mayer's (2003) book is an excellent resource for the perception part of the learning process, especially if you are using a multimedia approach for presenting material. They give a very clear and detailed explanation of the salient points, along with good reasons for the approach they recommend. We highly recommend reading both the book (Clark and Mayer) and Mayer's (2003) paper.

What Happens If You Do Nothing?

If you lecture and do not help students with processing, some of the material will be stored in long-term memory. After all, that situation happens regularly, and students still learn some of the material. Bjork (2004, p. 37) recommends "varying the conditions of practice. . . . When instruction occurs under conditions that are constant and predictable, learning appears to become what might be called contextualized. That is, while it looks very good in that context, the learning acquired in that context does not support retention later when tested in other contexts, and it does not transfer well."

This is a pretty damning indictment of constant conditions. But the real question is why does this happen? We conjecture that, at the end of a class period, some material in students' short-term memory could eventually be stored in their long-term memory linked to whatever else is in their focus of attention at the time, including elements of the immediate environment. In general, students perform better in the classroom where they originally learned the material. Changing conditions in any way decreases performance.

Psychologists dealing with people who witness a crime know that recollection is improved when they ask the witness to visualize the scene. So we know that something happens here that links perceptions to the context (e.g., the classroom, the course) in which they happen. As a quick aside, one of us had a situation where he had to remember whether a particular student was a junior or a senior. He couldn't remember which it was, but he could remember the student in classroom A. The seniors had taken the course he taught in classroom A, whereas the juniors had taken the course in a different classroom. Clearly, his knowledge of the student was tied to the physical surroundings and was highly contextualized. We wonder if the idea of contextualized learning explains the inability of recent graduates to answer the questions described in Philip Sadler's (1989, 1996) films (Chapter 1).

There is one well-established, relevant fact. Laurel Currie Oates (2007) did a long examination of Harvard's system for educating lawyers. In that paper, she noted that "when individuals learn a particular concept in a math class, that concept is stored with other information that they have learned in math classes" (pp. 9–10). So if you are teaching a physics course that requires knowledge of some particular concepts in mathematics, the material is stored linked to other mathematics concepts, and you will have to establish new links to the physics concepts they are learning.

Other phenomena undoubtedly come into play after students have perceived new material and are getting ready to process and store it in long-term memory. As we have seen, merely presenting material to students is not sufficient. If the material is to be retained usable, it needs to be processed so that it is linked in ways that will facilitate later retrieval. We can look at some examples of peculiar links that have been observed in children as they learn.

The Earth Is Round—Or Is It?

Vosniadou and Brewer (1992, p. 291) found that when children are first taught that the earth is actually round many of them develop a mental model for the earth that is pancake shaped. An earth in the shape of a pancake is simultaneously round and flat, and that is the way that they combine their new perception (a round earth) with their previous knowledge (the misconception that the earth is flat). In this case, the connection made only complicates the problem that the teacher has.

We should also note that there are technical terms for what happens in this situation. Incorporating new information into incorrect schemata (like a flat-Earth schema) is "assimilation" (Kalman, 2006), whereas generating new, correct schemata is "accommodation."

Fishy Connections

The National Research Council report "How People Learn" (Bransford et al., 2000) also presents another example. The children's book *Fish Is Fish* (Lionni, 1974) tells a story of a fish who has a tadpole as a friend. Knowing that the tadpole will grow up to be a frog and will be able to observe the world above the pond and report on that world to the fish, the fish gets the tadpole to promise to come back as a frog and describe the world outside of the pond. When the frog comes back, the frog describes people, birds, and cows.

When the frog describes a human with legs, the fish envisions a fish with a split tail that lets the fish walk. When the frog describes a bird, the fish envisions a fish with large fins that let the fish fly. When the frog describes a cow, the fish envisions a fish with udders. In all of these cases, the fish connects the new information from the frog with what it already knows.

You need to be careful at this stage and remember that students may well not be able to keep everything you present in their working memory. Material needs to be processed and integrated with material they already have in their long-term memory (assimilated) before it can be safely said that that material has been learned.

Summary

To summarize, material presented and perceived by the learner goes through two major sensory channels to temporary storage in working memory: (1) speech signals end up in the phonological (rehearsal) loop; and (2) visual signals are temporarily stored in the visuospatial sketchpad. Working memory is memory that is evanescent. Material in the working memory may not be remembered unless something is done to store that material in long-term memory. As you attempt to use the material from this chapter in a classroom setting, the following points should be remembered. Working memory has a limited capacity. If you give students a long slide-show presentation, their short-term memory will become full, and new material will be lost. Sweller and Chandler (1994) refer to this as "cognitive overload." Working memory is also temporary. If students do not do something that helps them to store that material in long-term memory, then limited learning occurs. We'll examine evidence for good ways to help students integrate material into long-term memory in the next chapter.

What's Coming Up

We are going to move on to the next stage in the learning process where newly perceived material is integrated into students' long-term memory. Your goal, at that point, is to get learners to somehow integrate the material into long-term memory, either by building a completely new schema or by integrating the material into pre-existing schemata.

The next chapter shows considerable evidence for the effectiveness of various kinds of active learning techniques, but the work has not necessarily been done in the context of the memory model that we have presented. Our approach in the next chapter will be to examine the evidence that exists and then to consider what might be occurring in the minds of learners when the instructor uses those techniques. In the context of the memory model we will need to critique some of the techniques that have been advocated. The researchers in this area have not looked at these problems through the same lens as the researchers who have developed the models for perception and short-term memory. In many ways we will be "looking through a glass darkly."

4

Processing and Active Learning
How Does It Happen?

The newly perceived material in learners' short-term memory is the raw material that will be used to reconstruct the knowledge structures (schemata) or to construct completely new ones in their long-term memory. If the new material is processed or integrated with what is already known, the result will be links or connections to material already in learners' long-term memory, whether the material in memory is true. Or new knowledge structures that use both new and old stored material can be created. Much of the literature seems to focus on how links are created at this point in the learning process.

Cowan (2005, p. 7) observes that "the focus of attention and its contents are of interest if links are formed between all of the information held in that focus at the same time. The way in which new ideas are entered into the memory system would appear to be that already known ideas are hooked together in a new way." Here the focus of attention can be thought of as working memory; teachers need to act while the new material is still the focus of attention.

A number of educational writers have noted that the integration of newly perceived material is critical for long-term retention and use of that material. We find an example of that in deWinstanley and Bjork (2000, p. 20): "Learning does not happen, for example, by some sort of literal recording process. Rather, learning is an interpretative process: new information is stored by relating it to, or linking it up with what is already known. The process is fundamentally semantic. New information is stored in terms of its meaning as defined by its associations and relationships to existing knowledge"

This quote really gets at the heart of what we need to work on in student learning. The "associations and relationships to existing knowledge" that we help students form are the most important aspect of learning. Isolated knowledge with no links to existing knowledge will be inert knowledge that learners cannot access to apply. This concept has a second important element. It explicitly rejects the idea that learning is a recording process. Too often, instructors work from the assumption that the goal of their teaching is to produce a copy of their understanding in students' minds. This cannot be achieved and is based on a "transmission of knowledge" model of learning.

Integrating Perceptions into Long-Term Memory—Processing

Learning is not just acquiring new facts. DeWinstanley and Bjork's (2000) observation points out the importance of "associations and relationships to existing knowledge." What students already know is bound to be different from what the instructor knows, and consequently students' version of the material after learning is bound to be different from that of the instructor.

Two different items need to be integrated at this juncture: the newly perceived material (auditory–verbal information and visual information), and the information already stored in learners' long-term memory in the form of various schemata. Newly perceived information residing in learners' working memory is not stored directly into their long-term memory without reference to what they already know. You can think of generating "hooks" or "links" (the term used by Cowan, 2005) to material already known. Or, as we've described it, you can think in terms of the new material being used to construct entirely new schemata or to rebuild schemata that learners already "own."

For example, if students are learning about various kinds of trees, then that material can and should be linked to material about other vascular plants. The richness of biology is related to the organization that we see in life-forms. Or if learners are working on a specific problem, it may well help them understand how material already known can be used—enriching by modifying current schemata. Working on a first-order chemical reaction should help learners understand first-order differential equations better. If learners are working on a particular operational amplifier circuit, that material needs to be connected to what they already know about operational amplifier circuits, especially to basic circuits like the building blocks in that circuit.

What Could Happen as Learners Process Material?

In Chapter 3, we visualized the learning process using the model shown in Figure 4.1. This model shows two sensory paths (and there could be a third path for kinesthetic/tactile perception.) for perception into two portions of short-term memory. This model also demonstrates that material from the long-term memory must be accessed and combined somehow (i.e., integrated) with the material in the short-term memory. In other words, the knowledge representations (or at least parts) in long-term memory are accessed

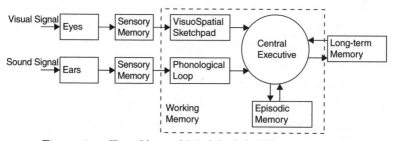

Figure 4.1. Two Channel Model of the Memory System

or retrieved (brought into short-term memory), and learners combine those representations with what has just been perceived, a process that rebuilds (or renovates) existing schemata. That puts the newly learned material into a richer context for the user as links with previously learned material are established.

Let's use another World Wide Web analogy. As links among bits of information on the Web grow in number and complexity, the information becomes richer, more meaningful, and more useful. When more connections are made between newly learned material and previously learned material, the former is more meaningful to learners and can be retrieved more easily when it is needed.

When learners process material, they start to establish links and to integrate the newly learned material with what they already know, but a number of things could happen at this point. The learner could build a completely new schema, which might or might not have links to other related schemata. If the instructor does nothing to activate existing schemata, then there well could be no links generated. If nothing is done to build links between the new material and known material, then the new material can be difficult to access. The knowledge is isolated and without context.

In addition, incorrect (e.g., containing misconceptions) existing schemata could be activated, in which case a complete reconstruction is necessary. Learners make that kind of reconstruction only when the new material is in direct conflict with the existing understanding. Or correct existing schemata may be activated, but it may not contain links to the newly perceived information. During processing, the learner could possibly either (1) build links to the new information; or (2) build new processes that involve the new information. For example, when learning about compound interest, new information about effects of compounding interest could be used in calculations of effective interest rate. The goal would be to build those new processes into the existing schemata along with links to the new information. And if the instructor lectures and leaves without any questions, nothing at all may happen, and the material in learners' short-term memory may simply evaporate.

What we need to identify are teaching strategies that will maximize the amount of learning that occurs. We surely do not want learners to lose all of the material presented in a class period or to begin to construct completely new schemata unrelated to their prior knowledge. Happily, there are teaching strategies that can accommodate both cases, in which schemata already exist but need some serious rebuilding and in which students link appropriately to prior knowledge but their schemata must be expanded to include the new material.

In Chapter 3 we noted that children—and other, older humans as well—can link new material to previously learned, but incorrect, material. The example was the construction of a schema for a pancake-shaped earth. Previous knowledge is important, especially if there are misconceptions in the material already learned.

Getting to the Evidence

Although the ultimate goal of constructing a particular kind of schema can be defined fairly clearly, the real problem is that most of the research on the topic does not specifically address this process. Rather, much of the research is focused on the effectiveness of various modes of teaching. Thus, we will need to read between the lines as we discuss the evidence and to try to establish connections between it and our depictions of schemata, working memory, and other aspects of our model.

The next section is intended to get you thinking about what needs to happen to the material students perceive. We have seen that just presenting material and getting it into students' short-term memory does not ensure that they have learned it. You need to guide students in a way that helps them integrate the new material with what they already know.

In thinking about ways to accomplish this, two questions should be considered. First, exactly how might you assist students in making links to material they already know? It seems fairly obvious that you need to do something that makes them retrieve some already known material and work with it plus the new material in a way that produces a new, combined schema in their mind. We will keep coming back to this question for the rest of the book.

The second question is less direct. You know that you want the student to connect the new material with what they already know, but what kind of learning do you want them to achieve? Asked another way, is there some particular kind of learning, or level of learning, that you want to achieve so that students will form links, remember the material, and use that material? Being able to use the new material when needed is an indication that the desired links have been formed. In a later chapter we will examine the concept of Bloom's Taxonomy of Educational Objectives, which categorizes levels of understanding including memorization (the lowest level in Bloom's taxonomy) through application to the ability to evaluate and make decisions using the knowledge learned. Working toward a specific level of understanding may facilitate link formation.

In the remainder of this chapter, we will look at some evidence that active learning activities help students learn better. Even though the evidence that active learning produces deeper learning than traditional methods is strong, much of it is correlational: It establishes associations but not causations. What makes it convincing is the quantity of evidence. There is much we could consider here, but we focus on a well-known and highly regarded study by Hake (1998). For a summary of the range of work done on active learning see Prince (2004).

The Evidence for Active Learning

Hake (1998) obtained data from over 5,000 students in high schools, junior colleges, and universities. The college students had different majors, although their learning was measured in a basic physics course. Hake found that interactive engagement methods produce approximately 2.5 times better learning than traditional lecturing. The study measured learning with a carefully developed and widely used concept inventory, which was administered to students before and after the course. The measure of learning was the percentage learned of the material not known on the initial concept inventory. If students scored at 40% level initially (at the start of the course), then they could learn the remaining 60%. If students scored at a 70% level immediately after the course, they had made up half of the 60% possible increase—moving from 40% to 70%, which is halfway from the initial measurement to 100%. These students would have a score of 50. Measured in these terms, active learning produced 2.5 times the gain compared with traditional methods of teaching.

Hake (1998) measured learning at all various levels separately, and there were learning gains at all levels. Even though active learning scores were substantially better than the scores for traditional methods, there were no active learning courses that, on average, achieved a score of 70. In the previous example, 0.7 × 60% would be 42%, and a 42% gain—starting at 40%—would translate into an 82% postcourse measurement (starting at 40%). That is just beyond the best that was achieved in the study. Finally, this study did not explore whether active learning experiences increased students' abilities to apply the material they learned.

Hake (1998, p. 65) defines interactive engagement methods as "those designed at least in part to promote conceptual understanding through interactive engagement of students in heads-on (always) and hands-on (usually) activities which yield immediate feedback through discussion with peers and/or instructors, all as judged by their literature descriptions." This definition contains a number of points that should be emphasized. In this definition, the caveat about hands-on being desirable and heads-on being necessary is presumably inserted for occasions when hands-on activities might not be possible. Here, Hake seems to imply that it is desirable to use both simultaneously but that when it is not possible then heads-on is essential. Hake also emphasizes "immediate feedback," either from peers or instructors. That is an indication that the instructor should be aware of what students are thinking and should take corrective action in situations in which (1) misconceptions are present; (2) students lack requisite background knowledge; and (3) when students put perceptions and background knowledge together in an inappropriate way.

We take Hake's (1998) call for immediate feedback to indicate that the processing, including the corrections, should be done while the presented material is still in learners' short-term memory. This is consistent with our observations in the previous chapter, and it leads us to some definite prescriptions for what the instructor should be working toward at this point in the learning cycle. It is also possible to give too much feedback to students—in effect trying to give them schemata instead of guiding them as they construct their own, an observation we would claim (not one made by Hake). What is astounding about Hake's (1998) survey results is the clear indication that interactive engagement significantly affects how well the material is learned; it produced learning gains that were over twice the gains of traditional lecturing in the study.

Concept inventories like the one Hake (1998) used are designed to measure knowledge of concepts, not facts, and conceptual understanding is important. The NRC report "How People Learn" (Bransford et al., 2000, p. 36) notes in reference to experts, "Their knowledge is not simply a list of facts and formulas that are relevant to their domain; instead, their knowledge is organized around core concepts of 'big ideas' that guide their thinking about domains." This seems to be a statement about the kinds of schemata possessed by experts in a field.

Once again we are reminded that knowledge of facts is not what to aim for if your goal is to move your students toward being experts. Even more interesting is that knowledge is "not simply a list of facts and formulas." And the goal is not a linear schema; rather, the desired knowledge would have links to core concepts, and students should be able to work with the material at levels beyond merely parroting back memorized information. Ultimately, our goal should be to help students construct their own schema but one that is close to the schema of an expert.

In the next chapter we will explore Bloom's taxonomy and understand the difference between memorization and higher levels of understanding. First, however, we will explore the basic ideas of *interactive engagement* more in depth.

Interactive Engagement

In interactive engagement, some form of active learning is being advocated. The type of learning described in the definition of interactive engagement is certainly not passive. However, we need to be careful, because not all activity that looks like interactive engagement really is.

"Understanding by Design" (Wiggins and McTighe, 2001) demonstrates how learning may be active but not "heads-on." In this study, third-grade students participated in an "apple" project (Vignette #2 in Chapter 1) in which they read "Johnny Appleseed," wrote a story involving an apple and illustrated it, collected apple leaves and made a collage, learned songs about apples, described and measured characteristics of apples, scaled up an applesauce recipe, and took a trip to observe making apple cider. "The work is hands-on without being 'minds on' because students do not need to extract sophisticated ideas. They don't have to work at understanding: they need only experience" (p. 21). The entire apple project assumes that a set of experiences is all that is needed to understand the subject—apples. In this example, it appears that "minds-on" probably means "heads-on." So it is possible to have active learning that is not heads-on. Chapter 7 contains a number of active learning techniques that are heads-on.

Reflections on the Evidence for the Effectiveness of Active Learning

Hake (1998) presents some very good evidence for the effectiveness of active learning, but there are some things that we need to note about that evidence. We don't want to minimize the importance of Hake's work, because it is extremely important. His evidence is some of the most powerful yet assembled to address the case for active learning in the sciences, math, and engineering. However, Hake makes no mention of the mechanism that actually produces the increase in learning attributed to active learning methods. In other words, he presents evidence that interactive engagement methods are more effective, but his evidence does not explain why.

An Observation on the Use of Statistics Without a Working Model

One of the authors once did some summer work for a company that involved a new magnetic alloy. The problem was to determine acceptable annealing parameters (e.g., temperature, times) to produce good magnetic properties in the alloy. After a small study, the results made no sense. After a great deal of detective work, it was determined that the annealing atmosphere had been changed. It was assumed that some details of the gas in which the annealing took place were unimportant, and no one bothered to alert anybody to the change. Removing contaminants from the gas actually produced worse results.

As an aside, we also heard an anecdote about a medical researcher who moved from Kansas to Kentucky, where he attempted to get his work going by replicating some of his previous work—using lab rats as experimental animals. In Kentucky, his Kansas results were not repeated. Further investigation revealed that the food (i.e., the rat chow) fed to the experimental animals was based on soy products in Kentucky, and the presence of hormone-like substances in the soy products caused the differences in his results. In addition, these hormone-like substances came directly from the soy beans used to make the rat chow.

The danger of doing a purely statistical study is that the researcher never knows if all of the important variables have been controlled and accounted for. There are often times when some variable is widely assumed to be unimportant, and then in some critical experiment that variable turns out to be the key.

When no explanatory model is used to describe what happens, things can, and do, go awry. As Petty (2006, p. 4) notes, "It is not enough to know what works, you need to know why. If you use a highly effective teaching strategy blindly you are most unlikely to get the best out of it. You must understand why it works to mine its full potential. When you teach you react constantly to the situation in the classroom, and it is your understanding of the teaching situation and what your methods should achieve that guides these crucial decisions."

Questions About the Meaning of the Evidence

In most educational research, some variables cannot be measured and others cannot be controlled. Hake's (1998) work is no exception. In light of this, some questions must be asked:

- Is some particular aspect or component of active learning responsible for the gains? In other words, just what is it about active learning that causes the increase in observed performance?

- Does Hake's (1998) study provide positive evidence for active learning and at the same time negative evidence for more passive teaching and learning methods, like lecturing?

- Is there some reason for the 30% failure rate for active learning? (Since the gain was, at most, 70% of what was possible to achieve and since no one achieved better than 70%, why was that? Is there some upper limit to what can be done, or are we missing something?)

• Finally, how long did this learning last? How well could these students use this material a year later?

Other research addresses some of these questions. For example, Prince (2004) contains a fairly comprehensive summary on the effectiveness of various kinds of active learning. As we examine various active learning approaches and search for answers, we need to keep these questions in mind:

• What active learning techniques have been researched?

• What exactly is it about active learning that makes it effective?

• What are the characteristics of effective active learning techniques?

• What happens in effective active learning? How do the students learn?

We raise these questions here because you will encounter a number of active learning techniques proposed for use in the classroom, and the only justification for their use is that they are active learning techniques. Remember the apple project: Not every active learning technique will be interactive engagement. These questions can help you select the most effective active learning strategies.

Summary

To summarize, after material is presented to learners and it resides in their working memory, it is necessary to integrate the new material with what they already know. They could build a completely new schema, incorrect (misconceived) existing schemata could be activated, or correct existing schemata may be activated but not contain links to the newly perceived information. Learners could build links to the new information and new schemata that use the new information. If the instructor lectures and leaves without any questions and without any processing, nothing at all may happen, and the material in the learners' short-term memory could simply evaporate. Then again, without really being facetious, that material could well be forever linked to the ugly tie the instructor wore when presenting the material.

There is compelling evidence that active learning (i.e., interactive engagement, heads-on) can produce substantial gains in learning when compared with traditional methods of instruction like lecturing. Presumably that happens because the material is better integrated into learners' existing set of schemata.

We have also raised some questions. Hake (1998) does not address whether interactive engagement produces learning with long-term retention or whether that learning will transfer to new situations. We will examine these important issues in later chapters on retention and transfer. To address them, however, we need a vocabulary, which we will get from Bloom's taxonomy. Ultimately, we want to use the evidence for active learning (interactive engagement, heads-on activities) to make a case for a number of techniques, but as we consider those techniques we need to understand that learning can be classified at different levels (Bloom's taxonomy), which determine whether retention will be long term and whether the knowledge can be transferred.

What's Coming Up

In the next chapter we are going to examine Bloom's Taxonomy of Educational Objectives (if you know it well, you might consider skipping the chapter). We will find later that memorization, the lowest level in the taxonomy, leads to impermanent knowledge structures (little or no long-term retention) and that working toward higher levels in the taxonomy, like application, can lead to long-term retention and, possibly, transfer. In later chapters we will use Hake's (1998) evidence and the concepts from Bloom's taxonomy to view and assess some of the well-known and widely advocated active learning methods

5

Bloom's Taxonomy of Educational Objectives

Its Relationship to Course Outcomes

In the last few chapters we reviewed how memory is organized. As material is learned, it makes its way through your senses and short-term memory into long-term memory. When that process is complete, you have learned the material and you want it learned in a usable form. Your ultimate concern is the form and quality of the memory structures produced in this process. Bloom's taxonomy (Bloom et al., 1956) offers a way to classify levels of knowing as well as to specify the quality of that knowing.

In teaching, you may have encountered situations where you sensed that students had only a very shallow understanding of material. But shallow understanding is an imprecise concept. Bloom et al. (1956) proposed a more precise scheme for classifying levels of understanding, and it proves to be valuable for a number of purposes. First, education is becoming more outcome driven. But outcomes should be precisely stated and measurable. One way to increase precision in outcomes is to specify where you want your students' knowledge to be in Bloom's taxonomy—this is where we start in this chapter. We've included an Appendix with information on writing outcomes using Bloom's taxonomy, which we strongly recommend you looking at if you don't know how to do this. Also, as researchers attempt to measure the effectiveness of various active learning techniques, they often frame their results using terms that fit Bloom's taxonomy.

Do We Understand What's Wrong?

Have you ever had a conversation like this one?

STUDENT: Professor, I don't understand my grade on the quiz on Monday. I clearly understood the concepts. I just couldn't apply that stuff to the problem on the quiz.

INSTRUCTOR: Look, your answer is way off, and from your work I can't see what you were doing.

STUDENT: I know I understand the concepts, and that's what you want, isn't it? I can show you. I'll tell you what *enthalpy* and *entropy* are.

PROFESSOR: You didn't work the problem, and I can't give you the grade.

STUDENT: Alright. I'm taking this up with the college associate dean for students.

There's a problem here, and we bet you've encountered it lots of time before. Students are convinced that they understand material. You give them an exam or quiz problem that requires them to use the material, but they can't in the way you ask them to. Then, if things go wrong, you can have a conversation like that one. What it doesn't address, though, is the issue of what the instructor might actually want students to achieve to be able to use the material later. You want to be able to measure, somehow, what it is that students know.

There are many reasons an instructor should want to have clear goals for where the students should be at the end of a course. Clear goals are especially important if you want to bring the students to a point where they can use the course material later in a different context. (i.e., you want long-term retention and transfer). You need to think about what that means and how you might want to define those goals—in writing. Bloom's taxonomy offers a framework that we can use to construct well-defined goals that can be implemented and then measured to determine if students have achieved them. Bloom's taxonomy is an important part of the vocabulary you need as you approach that task. And in later chapters we will discover that the effective techniques for long-term retention are also the very techniques that take students to higher levels in Bloom's taxonomy.

In the conversation with which we opened you have to wonder whether the instructor and the student are speaking the same language. Are they even talking about the same thing? We can start to figure out what the real problem is if we consider what is meant by understanding (see Wiggins and McTighe, 2001, Chapter 3). In the conversation the student claims to "understand" the material. Is the student's idea of understanding the same as the instructor's? Actually, that's a loaded question. It's not clear from the conversation whether the instructor knew what she wanted the student to achieve. But the instructor's lack of definition in that regard is complicated by the student's assumption that understanding was the goal.

Most of us think that we want students to understand the material, but let's ask several other questions. How would the instructor know if the student really understood the material? How would the instructor go about determining if the student really understood the material? How does the instructor measure something like understanding and then assign a grade to the student? Because trying to determine the state of students' minds (level of understanding) is so difficult, we ask them to do something (i.e., perform some action) that we hope accurately reflects their level of understanding, but that's really an indirect measurement of what they understand.

These are not easy questions, and there can be a lot of discussion and argument in this area. Part of the problem is that two items are inextricably mixed up here. First, *understanding* can mean so many different things, and, second, it can have different levels.

To students, understanding might mean memorizing the definition of something (e.g., the definition of *endothermic animal* or *vertebrate* in an animal biology course or *potential energy* in physics), and to the instructor it might mean that students are able to apply any one of those concepts to a specific kind of problem. Because students and the instructor are defining the word differently, they are not working toward the same goal. Both students and instructor should have the same goal, which should be clearly defined.

Understanding is not the only word with the potential to confuse what's involved here. What does it mean if your goal is for the students to "have a thorough knowledge" of the material you are teaching? What does it mean if your goal is for your students to "have a critical grasp" of the material you are teaching? We've borrowed these two questions from a discussion in Wiggins and McTighe (2001). And there are even more nebulous terms used to describe learning goals. Clearly, we need a more precise approach, and Bloom offers it.

Getting to Know Bloom's Taxonomy

In the 1950s, Benjamin Bloom examined the question of how well a person knew a subject. He discovered that there were different levels of knowing. In any given subject area, he found that it was possible to classify how well a person knew a subject area by how that person could use the material in that area. What follows is Bloom's complete taxonomy.

1. *Knowledge:* Recalling material you have learned; remembering, for example, facts, principles, or steps in a sequence.
2. *Comprehension:* Understanding the material. At this stage you should be able to explain what you know, to translate to new forms and symbols, and to extrapolate.

3. *Application*: At this stage you should be able to use the material in new situations, that is, apply concepts, principles, rules, theories, and laws to find solutions to new problems— problems you haven't seen before.

4. *Analysis*: At this level you should be able to break things apart so that relationships are understood. For example, you might analyze an amplifier circuit using what you learn about transistors.

5. *Synthesis*: You should be able to put together parts to form a new whole. Engineers do this when they write proposals or design new products.

6. *Evaluation*: Here you should be able to use what you know about a subject area to make critical judgments, to rate ideas or objects, and to accept or reject materials based on standards. The key skill is the ability to make judgments.

The steps in Bloom's taxonomy define six different levels of understanding. As you move upward through the taxonomy, you can think of that as defining higher levels of understanding. We would all probably agree that being able to apply a principle is possible only if you understand it as opposed to have just memorized a definition for it.

Now, go back and study Bloom's taxonomy for a few moments. We have some questions for you to think about and try to answer as we go along. Later, we will come back to these questions to reflect on how they were constructed. There is some interesting metacognition for you at the end of the question set.

Question 1: After you have finished studying the taxonomy list, close the book and on a piece of paper list the stages of Bloom's taxonomy in order. Check to see how well you did.

Question 2: Here are the stages in Bloom's taxonomy. Explain what a person should be able to do at each stage.

Bloom's Taxonomy of Educational Objectives

1. Knowledge

2. Comprehension

3. Application

4. Analysis

5. Synthesis

6. Evaluation

Question 3: This question is based on accreditation requirements from ABET, the engineering accreditation agency requiring that graduates of programs in engineering be able to do certain very specific things. If you are not an engineering teacher worried about accreditation, consider these requirements as examples. You should still be able to critique them (perhaps more objectively than those who must heed to them), placing them somewhere within Bloom's taxonomy as appropriate.

ABET Criterion 3 (Program Outcomes and Assessment): Engineering programs must demonstrate that their graduates have

A. An ability to apply knowledge of mathematics, science, and engineering

B. An ability to design and conduct experiments as well as to analyze and interpret data

C. An ability to design a system, component, or process to meet desired needs

D. An ability to function on multidisciplinary teams

E. An ability to identify, formulate, and solve engineering problems

F. An understanding of professional and ethical responsibility

G. An ability to communicate effectively

H. The broad education necessary to understand the impact of engineering solutions in a global and societal context

I. Recognition of the need for and an ability to engage in life-long learning

J. Knowledge of contemporary issues

K. An ability to use the techniques, skills, and modern engineering tools necessary for engineering practice

Were you able to attach a level to each requirement, or were you unable to find where some of them fit? For example, an ability to use some of the tools required in some engineering disciplines could really be an ability to perform certain motor skills like operating a particular piece of equipment, say, a lathe or an oscilloscope. Bloom's taxonomy speaks only to cognitive skills, not motor skills and not personal skills (other taxonomies cover those areas). So, there's more to this story, but we're going to confine the discussion to Bloom's taxonomy for now.

Question 4: For a course that you teach, write an outcome for one of the ABET requirements. We know you don't all teach engineering courses, but many of the ABET requirements could apply to almost any science, technology, engineering, and mathematics (STEM) discipline. Before you write the outcome, determine the level in Bloom's taxonomy at which you want students to perform for your outcome. Then write the outcome to reflect that level of performance.

What's the rationale behind these questions? We want to show that you can sequence questions so that they ask for answers that require knowledge higher in Bloom's taxonomy:

• Question 1 is a pure memorization task of the sort associated with the first level of Bloom's taxonomy, knowledge.

- Question 2 involves explaining something, which is a task that demonstrates knowledge of the topic at the comprehension level—the second level in Bloom's taxonomy.

- Question 3 seems to take you to the analysis level, the fourth level in Bloom's taxonomy. (We skipped the application level.)

- Question 4 asked you to use knowledge of Bloom's taxonomy to synthesize an outcome in a course you teach. That asks you to perform at the fifth level in Bloom's taxonomy.

This sequence of questions took you through several levels of Bloom's taxonomy, and each asked you something at a higher level in Bloom's taxonomy. Yet each of those questions concerned the same material—Bloom's taxonomy.

The Implications of Bloom's Taxonomy

At the knowledge level of Bloom's taxonomy, students memorize material. This, along with later recall of the memorized material, does not require that the material be linked to anything. Memorized material can be stored isolated from anything else students already know. The analogy is a file folder that contains nothing other than the memorized material. And, as discussed in Chapter 3, regarding memorization (e.g., lines in a play), there is a danger that you may get a knowledge representation that can be accessed only sequentially or that the material will not be linked to anything else you know.

At the comprehension level, students can explain material to someone else. This could occur with no reference to other material, especially if students use a memorized explanation. Only if the person receiving the explanation asks pointed questions might performing at this level require links to other material. In that situation, the pointed questions might require the "explainer" to develop links to related schemata.

At the application level in Bloom's taxonomy, it must be necessary to apply the material to something (e.g., a system or situation). This requires links to some sort of example system or situation, at the minimum. Depending on the quality of the application being used to assist student learning, there could be a reasonably rich set of links required for students to perform at this level, and trying to apply material should assist in forming those links. Using the learned material to analyze a system or situation requires that students have links (or develop such links) between the material used for the analysis and the material describing the system or situation and, further, that they be able to retrieve linked material.

At the synthesis level students are required to devise something—a system, a process, or an algorithm, for example—and the result depends on students being able to use the learned material on systems and situations they might not have envisioned or imagined previously. This means not only that the learned material should be linked but also that students should be able to establish and generate new links to the material that has been learned.

At the evaluation level students must recognize that the situation requires use of the learned material to make decisions.

When put in these terms, most instructors can see that students need to be performing at higher levels in Bloom's taxonomy. At what level does most instruction occur now, and how do we make sure that it gets students to those higher levels?

An Observation About Student Strategy Regarding Memorization

Maybe you are tempted to believe that students are really trying to learn material at a high level and that memorization happens only "by accident." If so, think about what happened to one of us.

One of us announced on Wednesday that a short quiz would be given on Friday. As it happened, there were numerous student questions on Friday, so the quiz was postponed until Monday. On Monday, after the quiz, as one student handed in the quiz she complained bitterly about its fairness. When the professor asked why she thought it was unfair, she replied, "Well, I memorized this material for last Friday."

Several aspects of this story are really quite appalling. The student was only memorizing—not aiming for any depth of understanding. *The student expected to forget the material* and apparently considered that to be normal. The nastiest conclusion of this story is that students care only about their grades on quizzes and exams and have little or no interest in any deep understanding or long-term retention. If you consider that many curricula have a structure that demands knowledge of material in prerequisite courses to succeed in later courses, then you might conclude that students expect to be able to relearn material in later courses when they might need it. They might also have the expectation that they won't ever really need much of that material. Working for long-term retention and transfer in this situation is certainly akin to paddling against the current, going upstream, and drifting backward when you let up. Even so, the goal is move students to higher levels in Bloom's taxonomy.

As you proceed up Bloom's taxonomy from knowledge to evaluation, the links between the material learned and everything else that students know are more plentiful and richer. They exist with almost no connection to other material at the knowledge– memorization level and reach a point where they might have to connect the newly learned material to their value structure. At the highest levels, synthesis and evaluation, students must be able to generate a truly rich set of links to much of what they know. Therefore, if your goal is for students to be able to use the material in later situations and courses, then what level in Bloom's taxonomy must be reached to assure this will occur?

The chain of logic that gets us to this question is simple. Students need to be able to use material after they have learned the material. If students are going to be able to use the material later, then that material needs to be linked to material they already know. And if that material is to be linked, then they need to learn that material at least at the application level. Memorization will not do, even if it is students' favorite mode of learning.

If you want the students to learn material to the application level, you need to work toward that end. You will need to specify exactly what you want the students to be able to do in a way that ties to the levels in Bloom's taxonomy. Our next chapter should help you do that.

As we address the issues associated with what students should be able to do at different levels in Bloom's taxonomy, we also need to realize that students need to perform at the higher levels in that taxonomy. In the literature, some interesting claims can be found addressing the ability of students to use material they learn in another situation later and the idea that the possibility of transfer is related to the level in Bloom's taxonomy. We address transfer in Chapters 9 and 10, but a couple of points about transfer are relevant to our discussion of memorization. When discussing transfer of knowledge from the learning situation to life situations, the NRC Report "How People Learn" (Bransford et al, 1999, p. xiii) says, "Knowledge learned at the level of rote memory rarely transfers; transfer most likely occurs when the learner knows and understands underlying principles that can be applied to problems in new contexts." The same report indicates, "While time on task is necessary for learning, it is not sufficient for effective learning. Time spent learning for understanding has different consequences for transfer than time spent simply memorizing facts or procedures from textbooks or lectures" (p. 77).

This is an admonition that our educational goals in our courses must be to go beyond simply memorizing facts or procedures, which means moving further up Bloom's taxonomy. If we want to get there, we need to be clear about what we want students to be able to do—and at higher levels in Bloom's taxonomy. As we write this, there is growing support for clear course outcomes and measurement of how well those outcomes are achieved. Though this is particularly true in the field of engineering, it is not alone in that effort. In the Appendix we discuss using Bloom's taxonomy to write and define course outcomes.

Summary

In this chapter we presented a definition of the levels in Bloom's Taxonomy of Educational Objectives, an opportunity for you to review and practice applying those levels, and some of the implications of Bloom's taxonomy regarding the structure of schemata as students learn material.

At this point we see that a reasonable goal is to at least bring students to the application level in Bloom's taxonomy, where they most likely have more complex schemata. They will then have a much greater chance of being able to use the material in later courses and in their careers, since material learned at this level is much more tightly integrated with other material in their long-term memory, with a much richer set of connections. The application level is a minimum, and getting to higher levels is very desirable.

What's Coming Up

The next step is to consider what has to take place in the classroom and learning environment to get students to the application level. We know from Hake's (1998) study and Prince's (2004) summary of evidence for active learning that the most effective approach is interactive engagement, or active learning. In the next chapter we will begin to examine active learning techniques, including their various permutations. In later chapters we will examine various modes of active learning as well as how transfer is tightly tied to students' knowledge level in Bloom's taxonomy.

6

Interactive Engagement and
Active Learning
Retrieval Events

U p to this point, we have discussed several interconnected topics. Hake (1998) offered evidence that "minds-on" active learning can produce substantial gains in learning. Those techniques have greater effectiveness, but we have yet to link that effectiveness with the levels identified in Bloom's taxonomy. As we proceed we will find that achieving higher levels in Bloom's taxonomy can lead to better long-term retention. This chapter begins by addressing a well-researched topic known as the testing effect, or the testing phenomenon, which can explain how some active learning techniques actually work to promote long-term retention and the higher levels in Bloom's taxonomy.

Some research on the testing effect or phenomenon is recent, but the findings are based on other long-standing research results. Our goal is to see how those research results and some of the popular recommendations for active learning fit together. Son and Vandierendonck (2007, p. 481) devote their book to applying the testing phenomenon in the classroom. Their first chapter notes, "For a long time, the two disciplines, cognitive science and education, have worked hard to discover effective principles of learning with the goal of improving educational achievement. And, although each has made significant advances, there has been a gap between the two disciplines, a gap that remains a reality today."

Regarding education and cognitive science, there seems to be a well-recognized disconnect between research and classroom application. However, the testing effect has long been investigated, and its researchers loudly lament why it has not yet been applied. We begin by discussing the testing phenomenon and its extraordinarily long history to appreciate that it is indeed very well investigated and also to understand how apparently difficult it is to get even a very well-researched effect implemented in classrooms.

The Testing Phenomenon

The testing phenomenon concerns test results. Instructors test students for two reasons: Either the instructor wants to measure what students know, or the instructor is trying to measure how well the material has been taught. In both cases, the implicit assumption is that some portion of students' internal state is measured and that's all. However, in physics we find the observer effect, often paraphrased as, "You can't measure a system without disturbing it." This is a consequence of the Heisenberg Uncertainty Principle. When students take a test, the system is disturbed, and after the measurement the system is not in the same state as initially. Interestingly, the observer effect is true in the field of learning theory as well as in the field of particle physics, and the system turns out to be disturbed in a particularly interesting way when students are involved.

The surprising fact is that *testing is actually a powerful learning experience* and not just a "measurement experience" (see Karpicke and Roediger, 2007). That's not what most instructors assume. But even more startling is that a testing experience is a more effective learning experience than a study experience of the same duration. A large amount of experimental work documents that conclusion; we now know that long-term retention is improved by repeated, spaced tests and that time on task is not as important a factor as was once thought.

The testing phenomenon has been known for centuries. As early as 1620, Sir Francis Bacon described the effect: "If you read a piece of text through twenty times, you will not learn it by heart so easily as if you read it ten times while attempting to recite from time to time and consulting the text when your memory fails" (Bacon, 1620/2000, p. 143; quoted in Roediger and Karpicke, 2006, p. 181). Bacon is saying that something can be learned better by fewer study events and more testing events. Trying to recite material you are learning is a testing event. You are testing yourself, but it's still a test. Bacon advises that students learn material "from time to time" by giving self-administered tests on the material coupled with feedback. During the intervening centuries, numerous investigators have worked with this phenomenon and have eventually concluded that the important item was simply how many times the material had been retrieved from memory.

A second mention of the effect can be found in James (1890, p. 646): "A curious peculiarity of our memory is that things are impressed better by active than by passive repetition. I mean that in learning by heart (for example), when we almost know the piece, it pays better to wait and recollect by an effort from within, than to look at the book again. If we recover the words in the former way, we shall probably know them the next time; if in the latter way, we shall very likely need the book once more" (quoted in Roediger and Karpicke, 2006, p. 181). James also gives a description of the process that includes phrases about making "the path more deep." He's describing the connection between where the perception is stored initially and what we now refer to as long-term memory. Today, we would say that the memory traces or links are strengthened.

Arthur Gates (1917) (in Roediger and Karpicke, 2006) reported on how the proportion of time spent testing affected the results. Using nonsense syllables and biographical facts as material, Gates found that retention (after several hours) was significantly better with less time spent studying and more time spent reciting (i.e., retrieving the material). That trend held through 60–80% time spent testing (i.e., retrieving).

In "Studies in Retention," Spitzer (1939) asked 3,605 sixth-grade students to read two 600-word articles on peanuts or bamboo and later tested them on the material. Some students took tests between the initial reading and the final test (which was 63 days later). The conclusion was that "tests or examinations are learning devices and should not be considered only as tools for measuring achievement of pupils" (pp. 655–656). This research has been criticized because the time on task was not equal. However, Spitzer's conclusion was noted by Glover (1989) in the same journal 50 years later. His work expanded on Spitzer's original findings. Recently, Roediger and Karpicke revisited the topic and did work that addressed earlier criticisms. Their findings confirm what Spizter found originally.

The testing phenomenon is rediscovered and researched, forgotten, and then rediscovered again some years later. Recently, especially since Glover's (1989) paper, titled, appropriately enough, "The 'Testing' Phenomenon: Not Gone but Nearly Forgotten," there has been another surge of interest in the topic.

Only some of the work on this topic is mentioned here. Table 6.1 offers a quick summary of the work highlighted in this chapter. It's not a comprehensive overview of all the work but offers a representative sample. The work summed in this table will allow us to examine some significant hypotheses about the important features of the testing phenomenon.

It's interesting how the results of one study raised new questions that were then addressed in the next round of studies. For example, after Spitzer's (1939) work, the obvious question was whether the increase in learning that he observed with an intervening test in the STT group was due to more exposure to the material that was not present in the ST group. That particular study was replicated by Glover (1989), but he included groups who spent an equal amount of time on task. Glover also began to investigate various time intervals between the tests. Roediger and Karpicke (2006) partially answered the time-on-task question by comparing STTT

Table 6.1 Some Experiments Comparing Studying and Testing

Year	Researcher	Summary
1620	Sir Francis Bacon	Improved learning by less study, with study replaced with interspersed self-tests.
1890	William James	Rather than studying, "recollect from within."
1939	H. F. Spitzer	Compared ST with STT and found that the intervening test produced better learning. But there was more time on task with S S T
1989	John A. Glover	S T S T T (ST) T S T T S (TT) T S T T T S T S T1 T S T2 T S T3 T
2006	Henry Roediger and Jeffrey Karpicke	S S S T S T S T S T T T S T S T S S T T S T S T S S T T S T Sn T S T Sn Tn

S, *study event* defined as a fixed period of time to work with and examine or study the material being learned. T, *test event* defined as a fixed period of time for a test using memory only (i.e., closed-book). S T, *study event* followed by a *test event* with time between the two events, typically a day or two. (T T), two testing events with little or no time between them; parentheses denote that the two events follow one another with no time separation. S S T, defined as *study event–study event* followed by a *test event*, and so on. T1, free recall test. T2, cued recall test (fill-in-the-blank). T3, recognition (multiple-choice). T, test of all material to be learned. Tn, test of material not recalled on an earlier test. Sn, study only material not recalled on an earlier test.

groups with STST and SSST groups with the same amount of time on task but with a direct comparison of the effects of studying and testing. The SSST groups were the best when tested soon after the last study session, but a week later the STTT group was clearly superior. The important conclusion is that long-term retention seems to be improved by repeated, spaced tests and that time on task is not the principal factor.

Since the effect is not a function of time on task, the focus now is on determining exactly what the important feature of these scenarios really is. At this point, the conclusion points to retrieving information from long-term memory whenever a test is given, called a "retrieval event." Simply put, the amount of learning is strongly dependent upon the number of retrieval events. In other words, the more often students retrieve material from their long-term memory, the better they know that material. Despite this conclusion's complications, it's important to understand its essence so that we can explore some of its implications.

This conclusion makes sense when you think about it this way. When students are tested, they have to retrieve material that has been learned and stored in long-term memory. So in reality a test is a measure not of what students have stored in long-term memory but rather of how well they can retrieve that material. Practicing retrieval by taking a test is practicing what will be tested and ultimately what will be needed to use the material later. Studying material is not practicing what will be tested because what is tested is the ability to retrieve material. In fact, studying once or a few times gets the material into long-term memory. Thus, the most efficacious thing students can do once the material is in long-term memory is to practice retrieving that material from long-term memory. Karpicke and Roediger (2007) address this idea. The more you retrieve the material, the better you will be able to retrieve that material on a test.

Emphasis on retrieval events is not restricted to Karpicke and Roediger (2007). "The single most important variable in promot-

ing long-term retention and transfer is 'practice at retrieval'"
(Halpern and Hakel, 2003, p. 38).

What Is a Retrieval Event?

We noted that these findings were not as simple and straightforward as they might appear to be. One complication emerges when
we try to define a retrieval event more carefully. For example,
Glover (1989) examined giving a test immediately after a study
event. The consensus now is that material can stay in working memory, and giving a test immediately after studying is not
a complete retrieval event because the material has not been
completely flushed from working memory. Therefore, it is the
number of *complete* retrievals, not the number of retrievals, that
counts. Partial retrievals can occur, which is why complete retrievals are called complete. Partial retrievals fall into a small number
of categories.

First, material may still be present in short-term memory
because not enough time has elapsed or because there has not
been an exposure to other material to refill short-term memory
with other material. (ST) events (Table 6.1) involve situations in
which the test is given right after studying, not allowing enough
time for the material to be completely flushed from short-term
memory.

In addition, material related to what is being tested may be
introduced into short-term memory. That material is often part of
the question itself. One of the more extreme cases of this is giving
a multiple-choice exam. Since the correct answer is usually one of
the choices, the answer has been introduced into short-term
memory, and students taking the test need only to recognize the
correct answer. We denoted this situation in Table 6.1 as T3. Not
only do multiple-choice exams give students cues about the correct
answer, but that incorrect information is also introduced into students' short-term memory. It is possible that the incorrect material

could be integrated with the correct material and could produce some undesirable results.

A less extreme case (a more complete retrieval event) occurs when less information is given to the student. A fill-in-the-blank question falls into this category, such as, "The capital of Alaska is _____." This situation is denoted in Table 6.1 as T2. It is still not a complete retrieval since there are some cues here, although not as many as in a multiple-choice test.

A partial retrieval might also occur when students recall only part of the material. For example, this happens when students work only on material recalled incorrectly (or not at all) on a previous test. In the simplest case, if students are attempting to learn a list of things (e.g., flower parts), the temptation is to test on the information not recalled in an earlier test. However, it turns out to be better to try to recall everything, not just a portion of the total material.

Questions that give no information related to the material being tested are referred to as free recall. It may not be possible to give no information whatsoever. For example, if students know they are being tested on the material in Chapter 7 in their textbook, that is a cue. It may not be as strong a cue as students would find in a fill-in-the-blank question or a multiple-choice question, but it is not a case of "no information whatsoever."

We also need to tie these ideas to the concept of schemata. When we say that students retrieve material, what we really mean is that the schema for that material is copied from their long-term memory into their short-term memory—much like computer data can be moved from hard-drive memory into working memory (i.e., random access memory [RAM]). We also understand that when material is initially perceived that it is possible to establish links to other material students know. In retrieval, one or more links to the particular schema need to be activated, and when the material or schema is retrieved (brought into short-term memory), those links (or memory traces) are strengthened by the act of retrieval.

That makes them easier to use when that material or schema needs to be retrieved at some later time. With the concept of retrieval now in place, we can look at some active learning ideas.

Testing Phenomenon Active Learning Techniques

A number of simple and widely used active learning techniques are reputedly very effective. One of the most popular is the one-minute paper.

The One-Minute Paper

This particular exercise has many variations:

- Ask students to write a short (two- or three-sentence) summary of points made in the class period. Students do this individually and hand in sheets of paper for the instructor to review.

- Ask students to write down the "fuzziest point," defined as whatever it is that was covered during the class period that students understand the least.

- Ask students to make up homework or exam problems.

Usually students are asked to do these activities at the conclusion of a class. But what about having them do the activities in the middle of the class, the end of the class, or in the next class period? As you're thinking about how you'd answer, don't forget the evidence presented in the last section. We'd like you to have an answer in mind before you read on.

You can also consider other questions. Is a one-minute paper a retrieval event? When is a one-minute paper a complete retrieval event? What do you have to do make it a complete retrieval event?

By now you should have gotten the message: A one-minute paper in various forms can be a complete retrieval event, but you would have to defer the activity until the next class period (which is presumably a day or two later). It will probably not be a complete retrieval event if you ask the students to do it just at the conclusion of the class, even though that's what is usually recommended. At the conclusion of a class at least some of the material presented or discussed could still be resident in short-term memory. That doesn't mean that asking students to summarize or outline the material presented is a bad idea, but whatever you ask them to do should involve representing the material differently or linking it with other known material. In other words, it should be a minds-on activity.

Considering Bloom's Taxonomy Levels

An activity like this can be thought of in terms of Bloom's taxonomy. For example, the one-minute paper questions can be framed as follows:

- Define momentum.

- Explain momentum.

The one-minute paper question can be posed so that students perform at different levels in Bloom's taxonomy. We suspect that there is a relationship between the difficulty of retrieval and the level in Bloom's taxonomy at which the questions posed to the student are addressed. When students are asked to synthesize something, then they need to invent something, which means many different solutions are possible. Not knowing what the solution will look like could well require retrieval of different information. For example, designing a bridge without knowing whether the bridge will be a suspension bridge or a truss bridge means that student bridge designers might have to retrieve information (schemata) referring to stress in suspension cables or information referring to the strength of truss members. It seems fairly evident that the cues leading to retrieval in a design situation or when students are working on an open-ended project are much less straightforward than the cues in lower Bloom taxonomy levels. It's harder when you don't know what you need to retrieve than when you know the general area of what you need to retrieve. However, retrieving higher-level material strengthens the memory traces more than if you expended less effort, and that material will be more accessible the next time you need it.

As stated earlier, the amount of learning is strongly dependent upon the number of retrieval events. Learning is also strongly dependent upon the difficulty of the retrieval event in that the level achieved in Bloom's taxonomy depends upon the difficulty of retrieval. This conclusion about difficulty of the retrieval event is strongly tied to the concept that the more difficult the retrieval event is, the more strongly those memory traces will be reinforced. Thus, the material will be easier to recall at a later time. Connecting this conclusion to Hake's (1998) ideas, the more difficult the retrieval event, the more the experience is heads-on for the learner.

A Simple Testing Phenomenon Application

We recommend not using multiple-choice (MC) tests; opt for short-answer (SA) questions instead (see also Kang, McDermott, and Roediger, 2007). MC tests have incorrect answers designed to tempt students. Choosing some of those wrong answers reinforces incorrect learning. Cued retrieval—as in a MC question—does not produce as much learning as a more complete recall—as in an SA question.

SA questions can be generated from MC questions. Kang et al. (2007) provides the following example:

(MC) What is a phoneme?

    (a) basic sound unit of a language

    (b) the sound structure of a language

        (c) a syllable

        (d) a cluster of consonants

   (SA) What is a phoneme?

SA questions take more time to assess, but they can produce better student learning, which is why we strongly recommend them.

Desirable Difficulties

Bjork (2004, pp. 37–40) advocates the concept of "desirable difficulties," or education methods that "seem to present difficulties for the learner, that appear to slow down the rate of acquisition, but actually result in better long-term learning and transfer" (Bjork and Linn, 2006, pp. 1–2). Because these methods appear to slow down the rate of acquisition of knowledge, they present difficulties for students, but they lead to better long-term learning, especially better retention and transfer. This almost seems like a paraphrase of the old adage, "No pain, no gain." We don't mean to imply that pain guarantees good learning. Not all difficulties are desirable, as Bjork properly notes, but some difficulties are desirable because they may turn out to be retrieval opportunities. Two desirable difficulties that fall into this category are as follows:

- Distribute or space study and practice. Don't cram. Short study periods spaced out over periods of days are better than one large cramming session.

- Use tests (rather than presentations) as learning events. This comes right out of the work we discussed in the preceding sections. The evidence cited there documents its effectiveness.

A Caveat: Retrieval-Induced Forgetting

Before we list three other desirable difficulties (Bjork, 2004), there is one caveat. Some evidence in the research suggests that when students are given a test, not only is the tested material retained better for later use, but also material not tested tends to be forgotten more easily. This is called "retrieval-induced forgetting." Researchers claim that retrieval of an item will tend to inhibit recall of related items. That is probably an indication that items not recalled in a schema tend to be inhibited. In other words, memory traces that give access to those related items are weakened. The effect may be temporary, and there are indications that those items can be recalled after a few days or so. Oram and MacLeod (2001, p. 742) note that retrieval leaves "unrelated and unpracticed memories unaffected."

This finding is bad news for instructors who test students on minor points in the material. They assume that if the minor points are learned well, then the major points of the general concepts are also learned well. In fact, the opposite may happen: the minor points retained and the major, more important points forgotten.

The Spacing Effect

We have discussed many of the aspects of the testing effect, but there is a related topic in the literature called the spacing effect. The testing effect comes into play when students retrieve material from long-term memory after enough time has elapsed for that material to have been completely flushed from short-term memory so that there is a complete retrieval. In the testing effect, it was found that the most effective learning events were retrieval events (testing events), not study events. However, there is evidence in the literature that even spacing presentations or learning events aid learning. As Dempster (1988, p. 627) says, "The spacing effect— which refers to the finding that for a given amount of study time, spaced presentations yield substantially better learning than do massed presentations—is one of the most remarkable phenomena to emerge from laboratory research on learning." In other words, students learn better if you take an hour-long presentation and break it into three 20-minute segments given days apart. And, as Dempster also notes, "the spacing effect is truly ubiquitous in scope. It has been observed in virtually every standard learning paradigm, with all sort of traditional research material" (p. 627). We will discuss this more when we examine how to apply these research results in the classroom.

Some Active Learning Techniques—Ways to Practice Retrieval

Felder (2003) recommends a number of active learning events:

1) Give the students something to do, such as answer a question, sketch a flow chart or diagram or plot, outline a problem solution, solve all or part of a problem, carry out all or part of a formula derivation, predict a system response, interpret an observation or an experimental result, critique a design, troubleshoot, brainstorm, or come up with a question

2) Tell them to work individually, in pairs, or in groups of three or four, inform them how long they'll have (anywhere from 10 seconds to 2 minutes), and turn them loose.

3) Stop them after the allotted time, call on a few individuals for responses, ask for additional volunteered responses, provide your own response if necessary, and continue teaching. We note that, by doing this, the instructor enforces a sort of accountability in all groups and individuals, since no one will know who will be called on to present—so all will need to be prepared to present.

We can categorize Felder's (2003) suggestions as either helpful for construction of learners' schema or as something that gives an opportunity for retrieval. We'll do this for the items he lists in his first suggestion.

- **Answer a question.** It is important to remember that questions can be aimed at different levels in Bloom's taxonomy and that questions at low levels will not strengthen memory traces as effectively as higher-level questions. No matter what the level, this will be a retrieval event. The challenge is to ensure that it is a retrieval event for everyone in the room—not just the one person who is called upon to answer. (If you do this, wait a few moments before calling on someone, or ask them each to write an answer and collect them.)

- **Sketch a flow chart or diagram or plot.** This is probably a retrieval event, especially if the activity involves creating a concept map as we've described them previously.

- **Outline a problem solution.** This is a retrieval event at a higher level in Bloom—most likely at the application level or higher. This could contain elements of schema building if students make links to other learned material.

- **Solve all or part of a problem; carry out all or part of a formula derivation.** Doing a formula derivation may be a purely mathematical exercise, and that material may be linked only to other mathematical knowledge. It could be an unhelpful retrieval event if the material is treated as purely mathematics with no connection to the material being learned (Oates, 2007).

- **Predict a system response.** This seems like a difficult retrieval event because there may be few cues offered necessary for the solution. But this could also contain elements of schema building if students need to make links to other learned material.

- **Interpret an observation or an experimental result.** *Or make a decision.* This asks for performance at a higher level in Bloom's taxonomy, and it probably requires a more difficult retrieval event.

- **Critique a design, troubleshoot, brainstorm, or come up with a question.** Again, critiquing is at the highest level in Bloom's taxonomy, and troubleshooting and brainstorming or inventing questions are one level lower. Again, this is a good retrieval event, but it is also more than that.

There are two major points to note here about Felder's (2003) suggestions: These are almost all retrieval events, and these retrieval events are at different levels in Bloom's taxonomy, some taking the students to fairly high levels in Bloom's taxonomy.

Not all active learning methods are retrieval events. Some of these activities put students into situations where they have to make connections to other material they know. For example, critiquing a design asks students to bring other knowledge to bear to evaluate the good and bad points of a design. That is more than a retrieval event. Consider E. Bjork's (2004) other three desirable difficulties.

The first is to vary the conditions of practice. Learning in different areas with different groups of people (study groups) leads to better learning than always studying in the same place with the same people. Learning becomes "contextualized" and will not often transfer to other contexts; that can be called place learning. Studying in a different physical location with a different group of people will make each retrieval event that much more difficult. A particularly interesting example of varying practice conditions is found in Kerr and Booth (1978) in an experiment with eight-year-old students tossing bean bags to a target on the floor. By varying the distance to the target, students were able to outperform students who practiced exclusively at the tested distance, even when the students who practiced at varying distances had not had any practice at the tested distance. This makes you wonder about how basketball players should practice shooting foul shots. They may be better off practicing from any point on the floor rather than always shooting from the foul line.

Another desirable difficulty is to provide contextual interference during learning. Paradoxically, a little apparent inconsistency between presentations can generate better learning. We'll discuss this in Chapter 8 in the context of a paper by Mannes and Kintsch (1987).

A third desirable difficulty is to reduce feedback to the learner. This is just the opposite of what every instructor has been told to do. It may cost you on your student evaluations, but it can, in some situations, produce better learning. And remember, in the work on study events (S) and testing events (T), the benefit is not a function of the grading feedback; it accrues even if you don't grade the tests, although we're not excusing you from the task.

These three desirable difficulties cannot easily be categorized as retrieval events. However, all of these three recommendations (including the recommendation for reduction of feedback) put learners into situations where they have to "think harder" to learn the material, to construct or reconstruct the schemata they possess.

Summary

To summarize, learning depends on the number of retrieval events. It is better to study, then test, rather than studying twice—keeping the total amount of time constant. Testing strengthens memory traces more than studying (testing effect, testing phenomenon). Some of this work shows that it is better to study for five minutes twice than it is to study for 10 minutes (spacing effect). Every retrieval event strengthens memory traces somewhat.

Learning depends on the number of complete retrieval events; partial retrieval will not produce learning at the level of complete retrieval. A complete retrieval event happens when sufficient time elapses (a day or more) for material to be completely flushed from short-term memory and when there are no retrieval cues. Retrieval of only part of the information—as when students study and are tested only on material missed in an earlier test—is not as effective as retrieval of all of the material.

Desirable difficulties should be considered as a way to help students construct more robust schemata: (1) distribute or space study and practice; (2) use tests, rather than presentations, as learning events; (3) vary the conditions of practice; (4) provide contextual interference during learning; and (5) reduce feedback to the learner.

What's Coming Up

The next chapter examines some particularly interesting research results focusing on active learning that promotes schemata building or reconstruction.

7

Some Active Learning Techniques
Studying, Retrieval, and Schemata Construction

I n the last chapter we examined some active learning techniques based on retrieval events. However, there are many other kinds, and their cognitive effects have been investigated. Of particular interest to us are those that seem to be designed to help students form useful schemata. In this chapter we will focus on some of these methods and examine what is known about why they work. Although active learning techniques are widely advocated and can be much more effective than more passive and traditional techniques (Hake, 1998; Prince, 2004), they have not been as widely adopted as one might expect. We wonder if part of the problem is that faculty have not been shown the underlying rationale for why they are so effective.

We see the following different learning techniques in use:

- Study-based events (typically not active learning events but activities that get the materials into students' working memory), including reading or rereading a text, lectures, movies, and slide shows.

- Retrieval events (which are active) can make study-based events active learning events. In the last chapter we examined some active learning methods that asked students to retrieve something they had seen or learned before. Retrieval events ask the students to retrieve material so that the neural links to the material are strengthened, thereby producing easier retrieval later and leading to long-term retention.

- Schema-building events are active and can make study-based events active learning. They have the goal of putting students in situations where schemata are built or reconstructed, adding links to other known material and enriching their schemata.

In light of these categories, this chapter examines some other active learning activities that have been researched and are advocated in the literature.

Reciprocal Teaching

Reciprocal teaching is an active learning technique specifically invented to provide better learning (Palincsar and Brown, 1984). The abundant research on this technique shows that it can have a substantial effect (see Petty, 2006, pp. 152–161 for a review of the research).

Reciprocal teaching has two stages. First, students learn the material on their own, which incorporates a study event. Then, they come together and teach the material to each other. In the process they have to make connections to other material as they present it to their peers.

An interesting aspect to reciprocal teaching is that the intent of the technique is to ensure that students engage in a specific set of activities while they work with the material. The following list provides the activities and identifies which category each belongs to:

1. Summarizing

2. Questioning (schema building)

3. Clarifying (schema building)

4. Predicting (schema building)

In reciprocal teaching, ideally two people in each group do the following:

1. Read the segment of material that is to be learned.

2. After reading the segment of material, a "teacher" is chosen. (Take turns on this.) The teacher asks a question "that a teacher or test might ask on the segment." Palincsar and Brown, 1984, p. 124) The other student answers or attempts to answer the question.

3. The "teacher" summarizes the contents of the segment.

4. The pair discusses the contents taking into account the summary and the answers to the question, including difficulties with the question.

5. They clarify any difficulties.

6. They conclude by making a prediction, usually about future content.

In Palincsar and Brown's (1984) study, the instructor initially took the role of teacher and then gradually turned over that role to the students. Palincsar and Brown emphasize the importance of providing a model in the initial stages, something that doesn't always happen when this technique is implemented. If the instructor plays the role of teacher initially, then he or she can guide students into more sophisticated responses by gradually getting them to take more responsibility for their responses (e.g., the questions asked after reading, the discussion that take places, making predictions). But if the teacher in the pair doesn't experience this modeling, that might confound the effectiveness of the technique.

Instructors do not always use reciprocal teaching in the same way reported by Palincsar and Brown (1984). Most teachers define the technique more loosely, ignoring that the original technique was heavily reliant on one-on-one interaction between the instructor and a single student. In the larger classes, and even in smaller classes of around 20 students, it is often not practical to use this approach, and we can see why instructors have more often used pairs of students instead of interacting with one other student at a time.

In these circumstances, the instructor should take care to ensure that the four activities—summarizing, questioning, clarifying, and predicting—are accomplished in the student groups and should understand how those activities are intended to function (Palincsar and Brown, 1984):

1. Students should understand the purpose of the material, including both implicit and explicit purposes.

2. Students should be in a situation that activates relevant background knowledge. It is important that students establish connections to the background knowledge that supports the new learning. We'd say they are constructing or reconstructing schemata. Activating relevant background knowledge means that preexisting schemata are the focus of attention.

3. Students should allocate attention. In other words, they need to focus their attention on the material being learned.

4. Students should evaluate the material critically. In particular, they should look for the following:

   a. Consistency of the material. They should get to the point where they see the internal structure of the material in a way that is consistent throughout. Generating that internal structure for themselves is a good way to link the material together to form rich schemata.

   b. Compatibility of the new material with prior knowledge and common sense. This works to establish links to other material or schemata creating richer schemata.

5. Students should monitor their ongoing activities to ensure comprehension by periodically reviewing the material being learned and by using self-interrogation, in which students ask themselves questions about the material as they go along.

6. Students should draw and test inferences using the material, such as by doing interpretations, making predictions, and drawing conclusions.

Palincsar and Brown (1984) also show how the initial four activities work to accomplish these six functions:

• Summarizing (1,2,3,5)

• Questioning (1,2,3,5)

• Clarifying (1,2,4)

• Predicting (1,2,6)

In short, they claim that all four of the activities require an understanding of purpose (1) and that all four activate relevant background knowledge (2). Summarizing and questioning allocate attention (3) by forcing both students to work on the material to the exclusion of anything else going on. (No headphone music at this point—there goes the "Mozart Effect"). Summarizing and questioning also foster monitoring of ongoing activities to build comprehension (4). Certainly, there is a strong self-interrogation aspect in the questioning activity. Clarifying demands a critical evaluation of content (5), and any inconsistencies should become apparent at this point. Finally, making predictions is clearly part of (6). If you put students into a situation where they need to make decisions, as in problem solving, they need to make predictions there as well. We'll talk about problem solving in the next chapter.

The Method of Contrasting Cases

Advocates of active learning frequently point out the problems with lecturing (Bligh, 2000; Wiggins and McTighe, 2001). Aphorisms like "Telling doesn't work" and "Wisdom can't be told" speak to these problems. Often, lecturing in many classrooms is a very passive activity for the students. It is anything but "heads-on."

However, Schwartz and Bransford (1998) claim that an instructor can produce a situation where lecturing becomes a heads-on activity. They propose some particular kinds of experiences for the students that prepare them for learning well from a lecture: "Suggestions for improving text understanding often prescribe activating prior knowledge, a prescription that may be problematic if the students do not have the relevant prior knowledge to begin with. In this article we describe research about a method for developing prior knowledge that prepares students to learn from a text of lecture. We propose that analyzing contrasting cases can help learners generate the differential knowledge structures that enable them to understand a text deeply" (p. 475).

This is a particularly interesting claim since this method is clearly one for constructing new schemata because it is assumed that students are missing the relevant prior knowledge. In that regard, this method differs from other methods that aim to work with prior knowledge, like the one-minute paper.

We cannot overlook students' prior knowledge for several important reasons. It affects their readiness to learn new material and could determine whether they are at a point where new material can be assimilated. In particular, prior knowledge is a large part of learners' motivation. For example, a presentation that addresses the issue of how to develop a winning high school basketball team, given by the most successful high school basketball coach in the state, will produce more change if the audience is composed of coaches who are not as successful. An audience composed of physics professors most likely will not get as much from the presentation because the professors are not prepared to assimilate the new knowledge. Schwartz and Bransford (1998, p. 477) state, "Students often have not had the opportunity to experience the types of problems that are rendered solvable by the knowledge we teach them. Under these conditions, we conjecture that telling is not the optimal way to help students construct new knowledge. When telling occurs without readiness, the primary recourse for students is to treat the new information as ends to be memorized rather than as tools to help them perceive and think." And those students have not experienced the types of problems rendered solvable with the new information. Instructors can, to some degree, control prior knowledge. They can require a set of relevant readings prior to class or can give a problem that can be solved using only the material to be presented in class tomorrow. Inability to solve the problem motivates learning the material when it is presented subsequently.

The quote from Schwartz and Bransford (1998) is particularly interesting because it essentially speaks to a condition that limits the learning. If students do not understand or appreciate the problems that can be solved with the material being presented, then there is little hope that they will effectively learn the material. However, if you can control a great deal of students' prior knowledge by preparing effectively before your presentation, even if the presentation is a pure lecture effective learning can be the outcome. However, not just any kind of preparation will work.

Schwartz and Bransford (1998, p. 504) present some experimental work supporting the idea that by using two (or more) "contrasting cases" students can build a partial knowledge structure (schema) prior to an in-class presentation:

- "Deep understanding requires both a differentiated knowledge structure (as develops when discerning the contrasts among cases) and an explanatory knowledge structure (as often comes through telling)" (p. 494).

- "Assembling ideas is important for understanding, but it is also important that people discern the distinctive features of the ideas they are assembling" (p. 505).

- "Generative activity is central to understanding, but the right things must be generated" (p. 505).

- "Contrasting cases provide a powerful way to help students differentiate their knowledge of a domain" (p. 506).

- "Deep understanding requires both differentiated knowledge about phenomena and an understanding of the significance of those differences" (p. 506).

Schwartz and Bransford (1998) argue that the knowledge structure (schema) at the conclusion of the lecture or presentation is what is important and that preparation using contrasting cases can greatly influence that knowledge structure.

Using contrasting cases to maximize the effect of lecturing seems to be a way to achieve the most essential element of active learning, the heads-on activity. In our discussion of active learning in Chapter 4, we discussed an "apple" project (Wiggins and McTighe, 2001) in which grade-school students participated in various activities related to apples, none of which were heads-on. However, consider what would happen if the instructor introduced a pear into the discussion. A pear is a contrasting case to an apple because the two have many similarities but some definite differences. Using the pear, the students could be encouraged to learn what makes an apple unique. They would be able to draw distinctions between an apple and a pear. (They would "differentiate their knowledge of a domain.") This is the kind of preparatory activity that Schwartz and Bransford (1998) propose. After trying to deal with the distinctions between apples and pears, the apple students would be ready for a lecture—or even just a short talk—discussing the differences, which might also lead to the differences between oranges and lemons, for example. In the process they would or could learn about the biological taxonomies involved, which would take their project to a much deeper level than would the original set of apple projects.

The same approach can be used in college science courses. First, get the students to consider two realistic but contrasting cases that will help them simultaneously see the differences and recognize similarities. The benefit of using realistic cases is that students are more motivated to consider them. They seem relevant, and understanding them appears useful. After the students have drawn distinctions between the two cases, the instructor is then at a point where a lecture can be used to help the students organize what they know. In effect, that is now the last step in constructing the schema for the two cases. Since there are at least two contrasting cases and students must resolve differences and commonalities, the resulting schema will tend to be more abstract than if a single case had been used in covering the material.

Making Lecturing Interactive

In an article on making lecturing more active, deWinstanley and Bjork (2000) argue that many situations seem to have no alternative to presenting material and little opportunity for students to process material, thereby engaging in schemata construction. Not everyone can teach in an intimate setting with 20 students in a class. With hundreds of students in a lecture format, it may seem that the instructor has no alternative but to lecture. However, deWinstanley and Bjork give numerous suggestions for ways to lecture in a way that permits student processing. They claim that for effective processing the following four components are necessary: attention; interpretation and elaboration; generation; and practice at retrieval.

Divided attention can be especially detrimental when students are acquiring material and processing it to store it into long-term memory, which makes us wonder about the evidence for the Mozart Effect. For example, slides can be destructive if students divide their attention between things spoken by the presenter and a slide left on a whiteboard or a projection screen. DeWinstanley and Bjork (2000) also note that many other things can steal learners' attention, including daydreaming and Albert Einstein's famous "elemental psychic forces." Finally, attention can be divided when students process material themselves, especially if they go back to their notes to study and listen to music as they study (the Anti-Mozart Effect?). The conclusion is that attention-dividing factors need to be avoided during lecturing when students are "encoding" new material, which happens when they are constructing links between the new material and existing knowledge. Interestingly, deWinstanley and Bjork found no problem with attention-dividing situations when students were trying to retrieve previously learned material, which may be a desirable difficulty. They also found that material learned when attention is divided may not be learned as well but that learners do not realize this and in fact think they know the material well.

The second factor is interpretation and elaboration. It is not enough simply to present material and assume that students learn it. The instructor needs to give students an opportunity to interpret and elaborate on the material—a first step in schema construction. Interpreting material means that it is made to fit with previously learned material. This helps students begin to make links to existing knowledge, and the instructor should assist with this process. An instructor should help students elaborate on the material by guiding them through the material's nuances and variations. Clearly, this factor is designed to construct richer schemata.

Generation is simply the idea that students learn better if they figure things out for themselves (i.e., self-discovery) rather than having the material presented to them, that is, when students generate the knowledge themselves. DeWinstanley and Bjork

(2000, p. 23) note that students can generate "new information, associations or interconnections from cues or partial information." Again, this factor is designed to produce richer schemata in the minds of the students.

Finally, an important factor is practice at retrieval. It is possible, deWinstanley and Bjork (2000) point out, to have students get practice at retrieval within a lecture, and they give some specific ideas for how to present material in a lecture format to provide retrieval opportunities. They recommend spacing out opportunities (what we've discussed previously as the spacing effect) for students to encounter material as an effective way to give students practice at retrieval. To help students make connections, an instructor can present the same material from different viewpoints. In mathematics problems, there may be more than one way to solve a problem or different kinds of applications. In engineering, a concept might have applications in electrical, chemical, and mechanical engineering, for example, and those disparate applications should be presented, even if the course is supposed to address just one of those areas. (An example might be conservation in flow, including fluid flow, heat flow, and charge flow.) Students will be better able to generalize their knowledge with this approach, and their understanding of the concepts will be richer.

Elaborative interrogation is the last technique in deWinstanley and Bjork's (2000) article and involves asking students to explain not just material but also why an answer is correct. The technique also incorporates posing real questions and ensuring that all students at least attempt to answer the question. That kind of engagement is surely heads-on and would be an example of the type of processing advocated in Hake (1998). We would expect that having to explain could lead to reinforcing memory traces to related material.

Overall, deWinstanley and Bjork (2000) give a compelling argument that lecturing can, in fact, lead to good learning, and they give a number of concrete approaches that can be used to ensure that students employ good processing as they learn the material. These concrete approaches also tend to incorporate many of the concepts we have already encountered. At this point, then, we have reviewed two arguments (deWinstanley and Bjork, 2000; Mannes and Kintsch, 1987) supporting the idea that lecturing can be made to be active and effective if it is carefully designed and the appropriate conditions set up.

Contextual Interference

Mannes and Kintsch (1987) shed some light on the issue of contextual interference and how it relates to schema building. Their study involves some experimental work on what are known as advance organizers. You are using an advance organizer whenever you hand out an outline of the material you are going to cover. That provides the organization of the material in advance to the students.

Imagine now that you are teaching a course and that you are at the point where you want to cover some particular material contained in a chapter in the course textbook. Here's the scenario:

1. You make up an outline following the organization of the material as it is found in the chapter.

2. You give that outline to the students when you ask them to read the chapter. In educational parlance, that outline becomes an "advance organizer" because it helps the students to organize the material in advance.

3. In class you give lectures that follow the outline perfectly. In this situation, this means there was no "contextual interference," and you probably don't get many questions because you are so well organized.

4. You give homework problems from the end of the chapter and work some in class.

5. You test on the material at the end of the segment, and students do well on your test. You're pleased, and the students are pleased.

6. At the end of the semester students give you high marks on their evaluations, and they comment on your excellent organization.

7. The department head and the dean read your evaluations, and you receive plaudits from them. Everybody is happy— you, the students, and your department head.

This scenario sounds too good to be true, and, in fact, it is. Mannes and Kintsch (1987) say that material learned in this way will be quickly forgotten and will not be usable when learners want to apply the learned material. Paradoxically, a more disorganized approach would enable learners to remember the material longer and to apply the material at a later date but would lead them to conclude that their instructor is disorganized, in turn potentially leading to lower student evaluations.

In a sense, the organized approach does not produce the learning that the instructor desires because too much is given to students. By giving students the exact organization of the material, the instructor provides a ready-made organization and a blueprint for the schema they need to construct. They have to do little or no work to create that organization, and without that effort it will never get created in their mind. Furthermore, the organization is linear and resembles an outline, which produces a schema that is linear with no links to any of their other knowledge structures and with no links to application methods. The entire procedure is not one that works to help students construct their own personal schema.

This raises the issue of what is known about how to produce better learning and what is a better teaching–learning strategy. Using advance organizers, Mannes and Kintsch (1987) set up experimental situations in which the initial scenario (as described earlier) was followed for some students (the control group), but an alternate scenario was followed for other students (the experimental group).

First, students were segregated into two groups and were instructed to study a text in outline form. They were not initially given the complete text (an article about growing and producing biofuels in Brazil). Two outline forms were prepared. In one form, the outline was organized in the same way as the text students would read subsequently. These students are referred to as the "consistent text outline" group (no contextual interference). The second form of the outline departed from the text organization and emphasized the characteristics by which bacteria can be categorized. This form was based on an entry in the *Encyclopaedia Britannica*. It contained some but not all of the material in the text. These students are referred to as the "inconsistent text outline" group (contextual interference).

The students were given one of these two outlines and were asked to study it however they normally studied. They were given two sets of questions and worked to answer those questions using the material and then with the material removed. Later, students were given the text (on growing and producing biofuels in Brazil) and a designated amount of time in which read it. After the presentation, half of the students were given these five experimental tests:

1. *Summarization:* Students were given 7 minutes to summarize the text.

2. *Verification:* Students were given 24 statements to which they had to respond true or false as rapidly as possible.

3. *Cued recall:* The text contained a paragraph about Brazil's novel way to use microbes and sugar cane to overcome the country's energy problem. Students were asked to recall in

writing everything they could about Brazil and its fuel situation (5 minutes).

4. *Problem solving:* Students were asked to suggest a solution to the problem of how to separate desirable products from junk by-products using microbes (10 minutes).

5. *Ranking:* Students were given six alternative answers to these questions and were asked to rank those alternatives in terms of their adequacy. Half of these alternatives were suggested in the original text but were deleted from the text they were given to read in the timed reading section. The others were poor solutions devised by the experimenters (5 minutes).

Two days later, the other half of the students were given the same set of tests in the same order as the first group.

Mannes and Kintsch (1987, p. 91) found that "consistent-outline students performed better than the inconsistent-outline on cued-recall and recognition tasks." In other words, on a typical test like the kind given at the end of a content unit or at the end of a course in a final exam, students who had been given a consistent outline performed better. Mannes and Kintsch point out that students were able to "perform" but may well have learned nothing if they were not able to use the material later. In addition, "the inconsistent-outline condition did not lead to poorer performance overall, however. Students in this condition showed superior performance on inference verifications as well as on difficult, creative problem-solving tests that required a deeper understanding of the material" (p. 91). In other words, they performed well at higher levels in Bloom's taxonomy. In fact, students who received an inconsistent outline and had to construct their own schemata were better able to use that material when they needed to apply it in more difficult situations, including situations that called for creative problem solving. For students who took the test after a two-day delay, performance was significantly better in almost all regards, including recall for students who used an inconsistent outline.

We could conclude that providing an outline that mirrors the text leads to better regurgitation of material on the typical exam (cued recall), but if you actually want students to be able to use the material a little inconsistency is actually a good thing. Mannes and Kintsch (1987, p. 92) note, "These observations suggest that not providing readers with a suitable schema and thereby forcing them to create their own, or encouraging them to structure information in multiple ways might make learning from texts more efficient." They make this inference early in the paper, and the results obtained in three experiments verify it. They also point out that "problem-solving skills do not depend so much on a well-organized textbase as on a richly structured knowledge base" (p. 94).

Here they are talking about the knowledge structures the students construct as they learn the material, and they indicate that the consistent-outline method leads to a "textbase" kind of knowledge structure—a schema that is simple, linear, and with few connections to other knowledge. The inconsistent-outline method leads to a richly structured knowledge base, which is a knowledge structure (schema) with many links to other knowledge and which allows application of the material. With no inconsistency between the outline given and the outline used, the knowledge structures of the students look much like the outline that they are given.

Table 7.1 categorizes these results in terms of where students performed on Bloom's taxonomy.

Table 7.1 offers telling evidence that the inconsistent-outline students performed better at higher levels in Bloom's taxonomy (evaluation and synthesis), whereas the consistent-outline students performed better at lower levels. We wonder what this says about the importance of knowledge at the lower levels when trying to teach to the higher levels. Said another way, students who had

Table 7.1 Levels Attained in Bloom's Taxonomy

Bloom's Taxonomy Level	Experimental Tests	Best Group
Evaluation	Ranking	Inconsistent Outline
Synthesis	Problem Solving	Inconsistent Outline
Analysis	—	
Application	—	
Comprehension	Summarization	Consistent Outline
	Verification	Consistent Outline
Knowledge	Cued Recall	Consistent Outline

contextual interference—the ones given inconsistent outlines—were better at the more difficult retrieval tasks at higher levels in Bloom's taxonomy.

Students who worked with the inconsistent outline were put into a position where they had to resolve apparent differences between the material presented and the outline they received. This kind of active processing links the material presented with related information from the outline rather than just receiving and storing a linear knowledge structure from a consistent outline. It also helps students create linkages and knowledge structures that enable better long-term retention and transfer.

The final conclusion is that it is vitally important for students to be actively involved in the construction of their schemata. Providing an outline and following it mechanically does not require students to organize the material for themselves. In all probability, the schemata they receive from the instructor (usually in the form of an outline) are linear, with few connections to other material in their minds.

What Kinds of Text Materials Are Good?

McNamara, Kintsch, Songer, and Kintsch (1996) describe some experiments in which the quality of the texts was varied. The title of the article best describes the question they were addressing: "Are Good Texts Always Better? Interactions of Text Coherence, Background Knowledge, and Levels of Understanding in Learning from Text." Their experiments varied the level of coherence in the textual material given to different groups of students.

To understand how the experiments were done, consider the following sample sentence from their textual material, which was drawn from two relatively disparate fields—heart disease and mammalian traits: "The blood cannot get rid of enough carbon dioxide through the lungs. Therefore, the blood becomes purplish" (McNamara et al., 1996, p. 5). As they note, "A reader can easily comprehend these sentences without ever realizing just why excess carbon dioxide would make the blood purplish" (p. 5).

McNamara et al. (1996, p. 5) generated versions of this text at three different levels of coherence. Their low-coherence text, for example, removed the word *therefore* in the second sentence, thereby removing the connection between the first and second sentence. As they point out, there are many "potential sentence connectives, such as *therefore, and, because, when* and *but*, and there are no linguistic cues that would allow a reader to choose the right one." This forces learners to choose the correct connective by making inferences from other knowledge that they may or may not possess. This makes the text less coherent.

This strategy forces learners to draw inferences using their background knowledge. A higher-coherence text would simply present those inferences in the body of the material. A low-coherence text forces students to draw their own inferences. In the process students are building links or connections between parts of the material or between the material and previous knowledge. That works very well if students have previous knowledge with which to link. In that case, there is good long-term retention. However, if students do not have a knowledge base of any sort, then inferences cannot be drawn, and they may learn little or nothing at all.

One interesting inference drawn from this work is that learners just beginning a subject benefit more from a highly coherent text. As learners get to the point where they have some expertise in an area, however, they benefit more from a text that is not as coherent. Those less coherent texts force learners to draw inferences using their individual knowledge base, which in turn produces a more usable knowledge base. There are some serious implications here about a number of topics, including how texts are evaluated and chosen.

If some of your students complain that reading the text is too hard, this may indicate that they are still novices who cannot learn well from an incoherent text. One of the authors often uses a book in his Control Systems course that is probably not very well written. In his estimation, though, students learn very well using that book, even though complaints about the book have been numerous. At times he has used another extremely well-organized book and has been dissatisfied with what students were able to learn. If students are complaining, they may well be learning more—even as your student evaluation results are plummeting.

The flip side is that if students are happy with the text, they may well not be learning much that is of value. Contented students could be an indication that students have a reasonable amount of knowledge coming into your course and that the text is well enough organized (i.e., coherent) that they do not have to expend much effort to read it. However, they may well be reading the text thinking that they understand the material and ultimately may not retain anything. On that cheery note, we will move on.

Electronic Slide Presentations

Some points made in the discussion about Mannes and Kintsch's (1987) results speak to what happens when using electronic slide presentations. Today, some instructors use advance organizers, but many depend on the organization of their electronic slide presentation to structure the material. If an electronic slide presentation matches the text, then we have the same situation as we have with advance organizers, although the space limitations of electronic slides limit the complexity of the underlying outline greatly and often provide no connection between different slides (different parts of the underlying outline). In general, the underlying outlines in these presentations are very simple, often having no more than two levels of bullets. That, in all likelihood, leads to very simple, linear schemata in the minds of students after absorbing such presentations.

Summary

To summarize, in this chapter we categorized learning events as study events, retrieval events, and schema construction or reconstruction events.

Ideas for Classroom Implementation—Schemata Construction

Some very specific pedagogical techniques discussed in this chapter can be used to produce an interactive engagement situation:

- Reciprocal teaching (Palincsar and Brown, 1984):
  - In reciprocal teaching, the instructor puts students in a situation where the following sequence of events occurs.
  - Students read the segment of material that is to be learned.
  - After reading the segment of material, a "teacher" is chosen. (Taking turns on this.) The "teacher" asks a question "that a teacher or test might ask on the segment." The other student answers or attempts to answer the question.
  - The "teacher" summarizes the contents of the segment.

- The pair discusses the content—taking into account the summary and the answers to the question, including difficulties with the question.

- The pair clarifies any difficulties.

- The students make a prediction—usually about future content.

- The method of contrasting cases (Schwartz and Bransford, 1998):

  - Students are given two cases that require the use of the same material.

  - As students examine the two cases, a situation is created that is a "time for telling." At that point a lecture can become a very active, heads-on event.

- deWinstanley and Bjork's (2000) method for successful lecturing:

  - Attention

  - Interpretation and elaboration

  - Generation

  - Practice at retrieval

- Mannes and Kintsch's (1987) approach (an example of contextual interference):

  - The instructor uses an outline (consistent outline) different from that given to the students (inconsistent outline).

  - Both outlines cover the same set of material, but the organization differs in the two outlines.

  - The learning (schema construction or modification) happens as the students resolve the differences in organization.

Though many other techniques can be found, these are examples for which research evidence exists. All the examples in this chapter share a common characteristic: They all require students to reconcile different viewpoints, whether they come from two different problems or representations or from the schemata of fellow students. That forced reconciliation seems to be a strong force for developing better schemata for the learning, and there is evidence in the studies examined herein that these techniques promote longer-lasting learning.

What's Coming Up

In the last two chapters we reviewed a number of research-based examples of active learning that tended to be well defined. In the next chapter we will visit a more "amorphous" kind of active learning—problem-based learning (PBL), which includes variations like design projects and extended problems. Substantial research in PBL justifies giving it a separate chapter. This type of learning leads us directly into cooperative learning, another important active learning technique.

Later, after we make our way through the PBL material, we will examine some deeper questions hinted at in these last two chapters, such as how students retain knowledge and how they develop an ability to use their knowledge in situations remote in time and space from the learning situations.

8

Problem-Based Learning
Where Am I Ever Going to Use This Stuff?

In the last chapter we examined general active learning techniques. Problem-based learning (PBL) is an active learning technique that merits discussing separately. It can be a powerful method for producing interactive engagement. In addition, a great deal has been written about problem-based teaching techniques.

PBL is an active learning technique that uses problems embedded in realistic situations. The problems may even be drawn from real situations, especially if the instructor has consulting experience or has worked outside the academy. Student activity focuses on using the material they are learning in realistic situations, which offers them great opportunities to make connections to other material and to build schemata that are particularly rich in connections. Those connections can be to other related material, to background material, and even to material related to the problem context. If the students need to make value judgments about their solutions and impact of those solutions, the activity requires students to reach the highest levels in Bloom's taxonomy. PBL provides retrieval opportunities with few cues that point to the material that needs to be retrieved. In the process, students usually get an answer to the question why—the first question in the Kolb cycle (Harb et al., 2009).

PBL not only provides an opportunity for students to develop connections, but it also can put them in situations in which they have to interact in ways that help them develop connections as they discuss the problem and generate or invent. solutions to the problem. It also helps students organize their knowledge a little bit better. PBL does many of the things that we want to have happening when we use active learning.

Finally, PBL provides a motivational factor not found with many textbook problems. When the problems are realistic, many students get the sense that the material they are learning has utility in "the real world," which motivates them to try to solve them.

A Historical Note

PBL was first used in medical education, but it has become popular in many science and engineering courses as well as lots of other disciplines. An early strong advocate for PBL (especially in engineering) is Don Woods of the chemical engineering department at McMaster University. He gives a short history of how he came to PBL in his chapter in *The Challenge of Problem-Based Learning* (Woods, 2001). One of the best books available is *The Practice of Problem-Based Learning* (Amador, Miles, and Peters, 2006). We will refer to their work as we go through this chapter, but we recommend reading the entire book. It describes how this diverse group of authors, each from a different discipline, came to integrate PBL into their courses, and it includes a great deal of their thinking about that process along with a lot of useful advice for teachers who have not used PBL.

PBL can provide a very effective way to insert interactive engagement and active learning into a course in almost any discipline, but it is especially suited to science, technology, engineering, and mathematics (STEM) courses where application of the concepts is an important issue and motivating students is always a factor. We start our discussion by looking at an "edu-drama" about using PBL.

What Is the Problem?

You may have heard a conversation something like this one. Ralph and Vladimir are professors at Barnburner College, and both are long-time teachers. We have placed this story in a laboratory course, but in truth it could be almost any course where the instructor wants students to be able to apply concepts from a course.

RALPH: I just got out of lab, and it was the most frustrating experience I've had in a long time. I gave them a lab problem that was a little open-ended, but all the students had to do was to apply the material I've been talking about all week. When they got in lab, it seemed like they had never heard a word I said in class.

VLADIMIR: I have just been reading something that relates to this problem. Let me read you a bit from this book *The Ideal Problem Solver* by Bransford and Stein (1993, p. 197). "An increasing number of educators believe that traditional instructional practice fails to help students acquire knowledge in a form that facilitates thinking and problem solving. They argue that most instruction is based on an antiquated 'transmission model' by which teachers and authors attempt to directly transmit their expertise to students. With the transmission model, instruction is usually decontextualized: that is, it takes place outside the context of problems that actually require the use of the knowledge gained."

RALPH: That's exactly what is happening in my lab. They can give material back to me in the classroom, but they can't use it in lab. That's got to be the explanation for why they act like they never heard of it.

VLADIMIR: There is a name for the phenomenon you are describing. It is called inert knowledge.

RALPH: Why does this happen?

VLADIMIR: They don't learn the material in the laboratory context. It is isolated from the environment where it was learned. The information is in their minds but isolated so it becomes inert.

RALPH: What can I do about this?

VLADIMIR: It is simple in theory. You give them realistic problems, not just exercises from the textbook. Put the problems in context, and use at least a few different contexts.

RALPH: What do you mean by context?

VLADIMIR: You make the problem part of a story that students find interesting and relevant. You also want to use problems that require using the solution to make a decision that has some impact on their environment.

RALPH: Where do you get problems like that?

VLADIMIR: Ah, yes, that is exactly the problem—getting good problems. You don't have to start from scratch. Start with a classical textbook or lab problem. You could use the operational amplifier exercise that you were using in lab. Here, I'll show you.

We're going to cut the conversation off just as it was getting interesting. We will get into how good PBL problems can be created a bit later, but right we need to summarize what has been going on. Clearly, Ralph doesn't know that learning is a two-stage process. He is transmitting information to the students (presumably he is lecturing), and the students are not learning the material in a form they can use in lab. They are probably just memorizing the material and operating at the lowest level in Bloom's taxonomy. That's a critical point. Ralph's students can probably give him back what he has lectured on if he asks them to do that in a quiz or exam—especially if the quiz or exam is in the same physical context as the learning situation (e.g., course lectures). The problem is that they can't apply it.

There is also a problem with the schemata Ralph's students are developing. Those students are not developing very complex schemata, and their inability to use the material in a different context proves that. Additionally, Ralph never gives the students a reason to learn the material. He's giving them material for problems that they don't yet know exist. Remember that "students often have not had the opportunity to experience the types of problems that are rendered solvable by the knowledge we teach them" (Schwartz and Bransford, 1998, p. 477). Schwartz and Bransford proposed using contrasting cases as a way to give students that experience, but the really important point is that students need to experience realistic problems because they need to know why they are learning the material—the first question to answer in the Kolb cycle.

In the problem-based scenario described by Vladimir, the problem itself is an example problem that is "rendered solvable" using the methods that are going to be studied. Problems should be designed keeping that in mind. We should also note that learning is "decontextualized"—taking place outside of the context where the knowledge would be used. In preceding chapters we have referred to knowledge as being contextualized when it took place and was linked to a context that emphasized a location like a classroom (i.e., place learning—as discussed in Chapter 6). Here, the idea of decontextualized learning seems to mean that the material is learned not totally out of context but in a context different from the context where the knowledge will be applied. Care must be taken with the concept of contextualization, since it has two possible meanings—the physical context in which material is learned, and the problem context we have just discussed.

The Problem Is the Problems

There is a way to produce better learning in the student. If Ralph used realistic problems, two things could happen. Embedding the problem in a realistic context gives students a reason to learn the material because they can see how the material could be used—that motivates them to learn—and it puts them in a situation where they will have to argue critically with their peers as they try to solve the problem. Both of those activities will help the students develop richer schemata.

But what happens if an instructor chooses a textbook and assigns problems only from that textbook? Textbook problems in STEM usually have the following properties:

- They are usually very well defined, which takes the experience of defining the problem away from learners, thus denying them the experience of integrating their knowledge. This may not be a desirable difficulty as defined in the literature (see Chapter 6.), but to us it would seem to be in that category.

- They usually have a single answer and often have only one solution method that works. More than one solution method usually clearly indicates within the chapter the preferred solution method. This removes the chance for students to make a decision about how to solve the problem, which might require them to compare different solution methods and deny them the opportunity for a possible contrasting case situation. This effectively limits their opportunity to link the material with other material.

- They usually provide all the information necessary for a solution. If that is not the case, authors provide hints that lead students to all of the required information, which is often in the chapter. That puts students in a situation where they only have to "turn the crank." In other words, they need only to memorize a solution algorithm and apply it. As a result, they are performing at a low level in Bloom's taxonomy. It is going to be difficult for those students to choose solution algorithms when the only problems they've worked are textbook problems. Amador et al. (2006, p. 13) note that "PBL problems mimic authentic, complex problems in that a path toward a reasonable solution usually isn't obvious."

- They usually have no extraneous information that would obfuscate the solution. A little extraneous information is often a desirable difficulty, which may make the "path toward a reasonable solution" less obvious, as noted in the previous point.

The properties built into textbook problems are usually perceived as virtues. However, that is not necessarily true. There is good evidence that feeding students a constant diet of textbook problems does not make them good problem solvers (Bransford and Stein, 1993, pp. 198–200). By doing nothing but textbook problems, students do not have the opportunity to develop a rich set of connections with existing knowledge. For example, if they are trying to solve a problem at the end of Chapter 7 in their textbook, they will probably thumb through the chapter until they find a formula with the correct variable solved for and with the given information and then will insert parameter values there to generate the answer. Thus, PBL does more than provide an opportunity to develop connections.

Students opt for this strategy first because it usually works. Second, given the large number of assigned problems, they must come up with an efficient strategy if the goal is to pass the course and get a good grade. Reading the text and actually trying to understand the material become an unreasonable strategy. After a while, students care little about their level of understanding and use this find the formula (FTF) to the exclusion of anything else. They often assume this is a good strategy. A note on one of our office doors says, "Professor, help me. I'm having trouble finding the right formula to plug the numbers into."

When students adopt an FTF strategy, they can usually do homework successfully and score well on exams if they memorize formulas. Often, such students will be the most successful in a course and get the highest grades. However, they are more likely to forget the material quicker than someone who worked toward understanding the material well enough to apply it to a real problem. Despite their academic success, though, these students acquire mostly inert knowledge (i.e., knowledge that can be recalled but not applied to problems) because schemata produced during learning are simple and unconnected—the kind built when students memorize.

Most instructors have seen plenty of examples of inert knowledge in their classes, like when students do well in the classroom but cannot apply the same material to situations in a laboratory (for more examples, see Bransford and Stein, 1993). These students are almost always stuck at the knowledge level in Bloom's taxonomy and are unable to use the material when called upon to solve a design problem. They aren't getting an education they can use, which means they probably aren't getting much of an education at all.

There is a "time-honored approach" of presenting "students with applications problems such as those that appear following chapters in textbooks," which leads to inert knowledge (Bransford and Stein, 1993, pp. 198–199). However, in many disciplines problems can be redesigned and placed in a meaningful context to help students build a more sophisticated knowledge structure. The following sections discuss ideas for accomplishing this (see also Bransford and Stein, 1993, pp. 199–207).

Connecting These Ideas to Consistent-Outline Concepts

In Chapter 7, we discovered that students using a consistent outline had better performance of skills lower in Bloom's taxonomy but that students using an inconsistent outline performed better on tests of skills higher in Bloom's taxonomy. Similarly, students who concentrate on solving textbook problems are working in a situation in which there is a strong level of consistency. The problems they work from the textbook use the material in the current chapter. Students working on less well-defined problems must determine for themselves what they need to know to solve the problem and often must define the problem themselves. These factors seem to provide the same kind of "desirable difficulty" as when using inconsistent outlines.

With this background we can now look at the issue of developing problems different from those in textbook—problems that require more student problem-solving skills.

Some Example Problems

The problems in this section are in pairs. The first problem is like those found at the end of a chapter in a textbook; the second is basically the same problem put into a realistic context:

1. Calculate the amount of lime needed to change the pH of 1 cubic yard of soil from 5 to 6.

2. Dr. Barnaby Barnburner is a professor of philosophy at North Carolina College of Knowledge. In his spare time—to adjust his psyche (i.e., to mellow out after a long day grading)—he grows wheat on the 160 acre farm where his house is located. He has just learned that his soil pH averages 5.0 over the entire farm. He wants to bring that up to 6.0 to maximize his yield. How much lime will he need? Oh, and you will need to know that Dr. Barnburner isn't much of a mathematician, so you'll need to present your answer in a simple, straightforward manner.

1. Describe the extent of the killer bee population in the United States using the provided map, and describe the effect of the killer bee population on mammals in the area of infestation.

2. During spring break, your family takes you to lunch with some old friends. One of the women, Annunziata diLuna, a county commissioner, is concerned because her county is adjacent to one where killer bees have just been identified. Ms. diLuna offers to give you a short internship for the rest of your spring break. Your task is to write a report that provides the information she will need to prepare for a possible invasion. She needs at least the following information presented in a professional format she can take to the commissioner's meeting in 2 weeks:

   • Possible provisions that can be taken to prevent or mitigate the invasion

   • A summary of ecological effects that will result from the invasion.

Both problem pairs involve exactly the same material and give students the same material to use, but the second problem in each pair is posed as a real problem, thereby helping to motivate students to learn the material. In the contextualized version of each problem, students need to apply the material, not just give a ritual answer from the textbook. In addition, in the contextualized problems that require a numerical answer (like the lime problem), it is possible to generate a formula that will give a correct answer for other values of the parameters of the problem. Requiring a more symbolic answer may be a better strategy. If the instructor asks for solutions using different parameters—like larger or smaller fields or different initial or desired pH values—then students will be able to determine how things behave. A more symbolic answer enables the instructor to use more what if kinds of questions—the fourth stage in the Kolb cycle.

In any problem-solving activity, students should define the particulars of more generally stated problems. Many instructors know that it is important for students to learn how to define problems. In fact, most problem-solving prescriptions found in texts admonish the problem solver to define the problem in one of the early steps. However, many courses, particularly in highly structured disciplines, use textbook problems where the authors go to great pains to ensure that the problems are well defined—often way too well defined. These are not necessarily the best problems for learning problem solving, especially for learning how to define a problem. Using a contextualized problem will generally force students to define what the problem really is, even if it is a textbook problem that is embedded in the contextualized problem.

Where Can You Get Good Problems?

Ultimately, you may want to devise some contextual problems for use in your course. Amador et al. (2006) give their thoughts individually in a chapter appropriately titled "No Problems? No Problem." Amador, from the field of soil science and microbial ecology, has an interesting perspective that sums up a lot of important points about PBL: "The problems I use in my courses come mostly from my own research and consulting experiences and from the problem sets I used to assign students in my lectures. I use the former mainly in my upper level courses in soil microbiology and soil chemistry. They are as real-life as it gets: messy, poorly defined, with more than one reasonable solution, requiring that information from different disciplines be integrated to address the problem—just what PBL is about" (p. 47).

As we showed in the sample problems in the previous section, Amador et al. (2006) also recommend putting a textbook problem into a meaningful context. They make a few other suggestions to transform textbook problems into PBL problems:

- Think of a context in which this problem might arise. Write a new problem in which the original textbook problem is embedded—so that students will have to solve the original textbook problem to solve the problem in context. See the previous examples with Professor Barnburner and Ms. diLuna.

- Use some humor in the write-up—as appropriate. Humor doesn't have to be embedded in every problem, but a bit here and there adds interest and can help to motivate students.

- Consider omitting some information, especially if students can easily find the information using library or network resources. Or the need for that information might arise only when students are partway through the problem—as in the operational amplifier problem that we will consider shortly. Provide it then, and blame its omission on the addle-brained characters in your story. Besides, that's the way life works, and students need to realize that frustration is part of most of the problems they will solve after college.

- Consider adding extra information that is not necessary for the solution but that is embedded in the story. If you're an engineer, chemist, or biologist, you know that rarely (if ever) do you encounter a situation in which you were given exactly the information you needed—no more and no less.

- Try to use problems that require decision making. Putting the problem in the context of a lawsuit, for example, provides students with an opportunity to make a value judgment, in which case they will be working at a the highest levels in Bloom's taxonomy.

If a problem can't be put into a realistic context, don't assign it. If there's not a realistic context, question why students need to know the material on which that problem is based, which should help you think through why the material is in the course and the department's curriculum.

Example—A Textbook Style Problem

Before we leave this topic, we'd like to offer one more example. We'll start with a typical electrical engineering textbook problem.

> Problem: In the circuit in Figure 8.1, determine the output voltage, V_{out}, as a function of the parameters, R_1, R_2, and R_3 and the input voltage, V_1 and V_2.

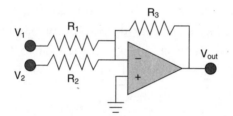

Figure 8.1 A Simple Operational Amplifier Circuit

This classical textbook-style problem is not really a problem. It's an exercise in remembering the formula for the output of this kind of circuit or in using a rote method for computing the output of an operational amplifier. Both of those operations ask students to remember something that was memorized earlier. If you use problems like this, students will learn to recall formulas, but there is little here to help them when they need to use the material on which this example is based.

Now, let's examine the same circuit embedded in a context that makes it realistic (and fun). This is the same circuit, and the calculations needed to solve the problem are also the same.

Dr. Abner Mallity has a problem. He has two signal (voltage) sources, V_1 and V_2, which come from two different microphones, and the signal V_2 is stronger than V_1 by a factor of two (2). (In other words, for the same applied sound source the signal voltage, V_2 is twice as large as signal voltage V_1.) He wants to combine these two signals to produce a composite signal where the two microphones produce the same effect at the speaker, and the circuit in Figure 8.2 has been suggested. He has been working with a rock band to help them solve some sound balance problems they've been experiencing. At his advanced age he does not appreciate their music and wants to get this over with as quickly as possible, and he needs your help.

Determine values for the resistors so that V_1 and V_2 both produce equal contributions to the output voltage and equal sound impinging on each microphone produces the same output voltage.

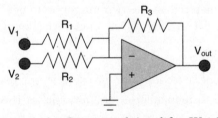

Figure 8.2 An Operational Amplifier Weighted Summation Circuit

Some hints to solving the problem: Define the problem. Write out one or more explicit problem definitions. (Your first one might not work!) It might be helpful if you could phrase all or part of your problem definition as a problem you might find in the textbook. After you have defined your problem, plan your solution. Visualize what the solution will look like. Sketch the process using a visual representation.

This problem takes students through the Kolb cycle:

- *Why?* The context gives some motivation for solving the problem—much more than a textbook statement since the problem shows how the material can be used in a real situation (e.g., adding two microphone signals). That aspect of realism makes students more likely to want to answer the question of why.

- *What?* The contextualized problem forces students to define what they need to know. The problem of two microphone signals has a textbook problem embedded within it; students will need to know how that circuit works.

- *How?* The students will need to know how to use the material to solve the problem. They must apply textbook material to the two-microphone problem.

- *What if?* This can come naturally in contextualized problems because the context can be changed slightly to change or complicate the problem. Consider operational-amplifier limitations or loading effects in the two-microphone problem. Possibly, you could add another microphone to the problem.

Consider how students will receive this kind of contextual problem. More ill-defined problems are not easier for students to solve—initially they may want to return to the easier textbook problems. The realism and humor may motivate them to give these contextual problems a try, but they might need some assistance getting started. It helps that this problem—derived from a textbook problem—is really a textbook problem in disguise. You can point this out to students.

This process is particularly good for single-solution, single-path (SSSP) or single-solution, multiple-paths (SSMP) problems—in other words, for problems that have one unique solution, even if there might be multiple ways to solve the problem. This is typical of the problems found in textbooks, and embedding those problems in a context produces more ill-defined problems. The problem solving can be guided by the instructor, who can coach students through the single path to the single solution in the SSSP problems. You don't have to start with problems that have 29 solutions, particularly if your students are at an early point in the curriculum. You can start with fewer solutions. But you do want to consider using problems that have different solution paths. They teach students how to make efficient choices and are worth using even if students initially resist this new approach.

Some Cautions

Using PBL is not without its perils. "If the knowledge learned is too tightly bound to the context in which it was learned, transfer to superficially different contexts will be reduced significantly" (Mestre, 2002, p. 5). When we first read this, we assumed that it referred to contextualized problems. However, it might well be referring to the physical context in which the material is learned. The context of the problem itself can be an important issue.

In addition, "students who learn to solve arithmetic progression problems can transfer the method they learned to solve similar physical problems involving velocity and distance, but students who learn to solve the physics problems first are unable to transfer the method to more isomorphic arithmetic progression problems" (Mestre, 2002, p. 5). This may well be an indication that generating more abstract knowledge structures promotes transfer so that students can apply that knowledge in different contexts and situations.

These observations indicate that there can be a problem applying knowledge if the knowledge was originally learned in a tightly bound context—like the problem with Dr. Abner Mallity. In other words, knowledge learned in this way might not be accessible when students need it in a related problem. Remember that material learned purely within the context of a classroom can be contextualized in the sense that it is also linked to physical surroundings—the classroom itself—and not usable in other contexts.

You can reduce that tendency to be context bound by embedding similar problems in different, varying contexts. In fact, the case for almost always having students work on two or more problems that require use of a particular concept in different contexts is very strong. You might need to assign only two PBL problems rather than a half dozen from the end of the chapter.

The real problem seems to be how the material is learned originally. Chapter 1 of "How People Learn" notes that students should "understand facts and ideas in the context of a conceptual framework" (Bransford, Brown, Cocking, Donovan, and Pellegrino, 2000, p. 16). In other words, if material is learned in a conceptual framework, then it is relatively easy to link that material to particular aspects of a problem. However, if material is learned within a problem, then linking that material to other problems may be difficult. The latter assumes that the instructor did not step back and help students understand the concepts embedded in the problem. This difficulty underscores the idea that a conceptual framework is necessary. An abstract schema for the material is the key to being able to use the material in a wider set of contexts.

These observations indicate that the order in which you do things is critically important. There are many times when learning concepts first is important. For example, we require students to take courses in mathematics before they take the engineering or science courses that require them to use that material. However, learning concepts in the beginning math courses in situations where students do not see where they can apply them diminishes their motivation.

However, once students learn concepts, it is also important that they apply them to actual problems without a large time between; this is important for creating strong links to the concepts from material associated with their application. As we take up the topic of transfer, we will find some work indicating that the timing of retrieval of learned information stored in long-term memory is important. Recall what we had to say about spaced retrieval earlier.

There is one final point to note. Students should reflect on what is happening as they learn concepts; this is an important metacognitive activity that is recommended by Bransford et al. (2000) (see Chapter 1 in this volume) in its three key concepts for improving instruction. As students reflect on the idea of learning conceptual material to be applied later, they understand what is happening as they learn those concepts and are better able to apply that material when needed.

None of what we've just discussed rules out using PBL cases and problems, but it does mean that instructors need to understand that timing is paramount. As we shall see in the next section, there are a few other issues of concern as well.

What Makes a Good Problem?

When dealing with problem-based learning we need to consider the complete learning cycle and the kinds of problem situations that make good problems. If you give students a problem, the solution might require more than they know at that point. A problem can and should be a learning experience, and you might well give students one for which they are not quite prepared. Doing so means you have to figure out how to present the material they don't yet know but need to know to generate a solution. Should you let them figure it out in the context of the problem? Should you give a formal lecture on the material? To answer these questions, we need to review the learning cycle.

In the model we have been using, the following stages occur:

- There is some prior knowledge that students–learners have.

- A *Time for Telling* (Schwartz and Bransford, 1998) advocates that the instructor manipulate the prior knowledge of students in a way that provides them with appropriate prior knowledge.

- Learners perceive some new material, possibly through a lecture or presentation by the instructor.

- Learners link that new material with the preexisting prior knowledge, forming either a new knowledge structure (schema) or modifying a preexisting knowledge structure.

- That new or modified schema is stored in long-term memory.

These stages are repeated as students learn more about some particular topic, possibly resulting in a growing, ever more complex knowledge structure.

In considering this model, we have a tendency to overlook the importance of prior knowledge that students bring. Prior knowledge affects students' readiness to learn new material and can determine whether they are at a point where new material can be assimilated. Prior knowledge is also a large determiner of students' motivation. Schwartz and Bransford (1998, p. 477) state, "Students often have not had the opportunity to experience the types of problems that are rendered solvable by the knowledge we teach them. Under these conditions, we conjecture that telling is not the optimal way to help students construct new knowledge. When telling occurs without readiness, the primary recourse for students is to treat the new information as something to be memorized rather than as tools to help them perceive and think." This is an especially important connection. Students may need to have a problem "on the table" to motivate them when we start to teach them solution methods.

Prior knowledge is, at least, partially under the control of the instructor. An instructor can require a set of relevant readings prior to class. An instructor can give a problem that can be solved using only the material he or she presents. Not being able to solve the problem may motivate students to learn the material that is being presented, provided that it is relevant to the problem they need to solve.

Schwartz and Bransford's (1998) previous statement is interesting because it essentially speaks to a condition that limits learning. If students do not understand or appreciate the problems that can be solved with the material being presented, then there may be little hope that the material will be learned effectively. Knowing the problems you've been assigned can be solved with the material the instructor is giving you greatly improves motivation. If students have some personal experience with the problem, that also helps their motivation. It all depends upon what they bring to the presentation stage of the learning cycle. But don't forget that an instructor can control a great deal of students' prior knowledge by effectively preparing them beforehand. In Chapter 7, we introduced and recommended contrasting cases as one technique that effectively prepares students for learning, and PBL presents many opportunities to use contrasting cases.

Because these contrasting cases have to be devised—which is no easy task—in developing the problem try to set up a situation in which students have to choose between two contrasting possibilities. For example, imagine that you are teaching bridge design. You could give students two proposals for a bridge. Those proposals could be for similar bridges or completely different kinds. In either case, have students be in the position of evaluating those proposals, and ask them for a decision on which design to fund. Note that you are asking them to work at a very high level in Bloom's taxonomy when you do this.

Whatever the problem that you use, you can almost always "tweak" it so that some detail is changed, and frequently that will change the solution. In that way, you can get students to compare the two situations and to extract the significant differences between the two situations.

After students have worked on the two contrasting cases for a while, then a lecture is appropriate. "Well differentiated knowledge structures set the stage for learning through telling but usually do not replace it" (Schwartz and Bransford, 1998, p. 481).

Putting It All together

Let's assume that you have decided to try using PBL. What should you expect? Woods (2001) presents some cautionary tales. In the first chapter he points out that students know how to solve textbook problems; PBL is less comfortable, so if the instructor begins using this technique they often resist. The instructor needs to prepare students for the change by ensuring that they are aware of the difference between the types of learning and the reason PBL has been chosen. This will help the transition and will also produce some metacognition since students will be thinking about their attitudes and approaches to PBL. Woods also points out that some students are not going to transition well to PBL, regardless of how well they are prepared.

Some time ago, William G. Perry (described in Wankat, 2002, pp. 161–166) proposed that students develop gradually along a scale starting with a very authoritarian view of the instructor. In this stage, students see the instructor as the authority and expect the instructor to deliver the information. The instructor is the expert, knows the material, and should teach it to students. In this stage (dualism), everything is black and white.

As students develop, they go through other stages of intellectual development, listed as follows, along with a short description of student attitudes at each stage. For a more detailed description of each stage see Wankat (2002, pp. 161–166):

- Dualism: There is a right and a wrong.

- Multiplicity: There can be more than one answer to a question.

- Relativism: Everything is relative.

- Commitment within relativism: Ready for independent work.

Only after some intellectual development are students at the stage where the instructor is viewed as a guide and a resource person, not as a person who knows "the answers." Intellectually, students move along a continuum, starting with the idea that all knowledge is black and white and the teacher is the authority and moving to the idea that some questions might have many answers and that the teacher can be, at most, a guide.

Many students, especially those in their first year or so, are at a stage of intellectual development where they are not prepared for the lack of definition inherently a part of good PBL problems. They are also not ready to work through problems with their peers when the course is being taught by an instructor who knows the answer but isn't sharing that knowledge with them. The role of the faculty member is to foster students' intellectual development, even if that means that he or she also has some development work to do.

Finally, PBL leads naturally to situations where students have to work together to solve problems, because it often involves problems that are more difficult than typical textbook problems, especially those that become semester-long projects. From these collaborative experiences students can learn important lessons about working with others.

Collaborative and Cooperative Learning

The techniques in this book are best used in settings where students engage each other as they work through the material. (That's built into reciprocal teaching, for example, and grows naturally out of PBL work.) It is certainly possible for students to work individually on problems, even contextual ones, but when they do they miss some of the most important benefits obtained from PBL. Hake's (1998) evidence focuses on "interactive engagement"— heads-on and hands-on. As students work in groups, they inevitably encounter misunderstandings and slight confusions, which force them to devise explanations and to fill in gaps in their knowledge, thus encouraging the kind of mental engagement that helps them understand the concepts underlying the project.

Collaborative Learning

Collaborative learning occurs when group members work together constructing knowledge. As students explore, develop, and then defend their conceptions they build or reconstruct schemata to produce richer, more expert-like, schemata. There aren't a lot of rules governing how the groups must function in this type of learning.

Most active learning methods are best implemented in collaborative settings. Many retrieval-based methods can even be made into group tasks; for example, students can be asked to generate an exam question collaboratively. However, many instructors are wary of collaborative methods; they worry whether all students will contribute their share in a group and whether the group will hold them accountable when they do not. One kind of group work called cooperative learning offers a way to solve these worries.

Unlike collaboration learning, where groups function without much in the way of rules, cooperative learning prescribes how students work together.

Cooperative Learning

Cooperative learning includes five features that eliminate some of the problems with purely collaborative learning:

- Positive mutual interdependence

- Face-to-face promotive interaction

- Individual accountability

- Team skills development

- Regular group processing assessment

Two of these features are particularly important for good schemata construction activity. Positive mutual interdependence means that all members of the group depend on each other for learning. There are no hitchhikers or stars. All members of the group work together so that every member learns the material. The instructor can design activities that increase this interdependence. For example, the instructor can assign homework and then randomly choose a member of the group to solve one of the problems on the board. The second important feature, individual accountability, means making sure that every student does work that is graded individually. Assignments are designed so that each student is responsible for a designated part and they are graded on that part. We all probably do this already, but the simplest way to hold individuals accountable is to give individual exams and quizzes on the material that was done in the cooperative group. We all probably do that already.

Advocates of cooperative learning are not in favor of giving group grades, but many of us in science and engineering do that for things like laboratory reports. Kaufman, Felder, and Fuller (2000) give a peer-rating scheme that helps in assessing individual contributions to team/group efforts (e.g., lab reports). They devised a form (available in their paper) that asks all team members to rate their peers and themselves on a nine-level scale: Excellent, Very Good, Satisfactory, Ordinary, Marginal, Deficient, Unsatisfactory, Superficial, and No-Show. Their scale of verbal qualities (measures of performance given by peers) can be converted to a numerical scale (e.g., Excellent = 100, No-Show = 0), and then grades for a group report or lab report can be adjusted using that scale. (Give the assigned grade to someone who gets the average rating for the group, and move the grade up or down depending upon the peer rating. That makes the grades relative to where students are within the group—keeping the average grade very near to the grade you assign.) An Internet search on "peer ratings in cooperative learning teams" yields a number of other good ideas.

There are various ways to assess how well individuals worked within the group, and they are not all that time-consuming. If an instructor has to grade only one lab report for each group, then even after factoring in the work to adjust individual grades there will be less grading than if lab reports are graded individually.

We've had good luck with another strategy. We give some reward unrelated to grades to the lab group with the highest score on an exam or quiz. A box of doughnut holes works nicely, and lab groups will work diligently to get that box of doughnut holes and distribute them. The winners often like to make the losers beg for one of the holes. The treats have little monetary or intrinsic value, but the value of the power to distribute them should not be underestimated. The reward does not have to be grade related to be effective.

Team Skills Development

Engineering accreditation criteria include a requirement that graduates should be able to function on teams. When a graduate is engaged in the practice of engineering, it is often in a team environment, and development of team skills is very important. Let's face it: if the group is dysfunctional, it can interfere with students' learning. We will see none of the advantages of interactive engagement and active learning if group functioning gets in the way of learning. It is the instructor's responsibility jointly with the team members to do as much as possible to ensure well-functioning teams. Good design assignments and attention to small group dynamics helps groups to function like teams.

Cooperative learning literature addresses the development of team skills in the individuals in the group. Several particular areas contribute to a group's effectiveness:

- Students should learn to trust others in the team.

- Students should support others in the team.

- Students should be able to communicate with others in the team.

- Students should be able to resolve conflicts within the team.

Instructors who try to develop team skills may have students engage in "trust exercises" of the sort often used in theatrical productions.

At a minimum, students should know what to expect of a team. Handouts about the Tuckman model, which outlines the four stages in group interaction, are often helpful (Stein and Hurd, 2000):

- *Forming:* Teams go through a formative stage. At this point there is some jostling for leadership roles and recognition as a leader, but basically team members are polite and are "feeling each other out."

- *Storming:* In this stage real jostling for leadership roles and recognition occurs, and teams can experience serious conflict. They can become stuck in this stage and never get any further, thus becoming dysfunctional. If this occurs the instructor should take steps to resolve that issue and get the team moving to the next stage.

- *Norming:* At this stage the team begins to perform as a team. There is no guarantee that teams will make it this far. It takes time, so, for example, a team formed for a two-week project will probably never get here. If you want teams to begin to perform as a team you will need longer projects that allow time for them to develop to this stage.

- *Performing:* Here teams perform really well—much better than the instructor might expect from the individuals forming the team. Here the whole is truly greater than the sum of its parts, and teams that reach this stage accomplish far more than any of the individuals within the team could have done working alone. This is the stage that you hope but don't expect all teams reach.

You can encourage teams in the following ways to help them get through the various stages:

- In the first team meeting, agree on a name for the team. This can be a good exercise to help students learn about each other, and creating an identity is one of the steps on the path to being a team.

- The team should agree to set meeting times in a standard way. In any given group, some students will work, some will commute, and some will be involved in a variety of activities on and off campus. Students in the team can argue endlessly over meeting times unless they decide on a way to set them up.

- Teams don't always work out, and procedures should be established for resigning from the team and firing someone from the team, including some time for mulling it over and trying to negotiate a way to avoid either of those actions. If, despite efforts to the contrary, someone is fired or resigns, then the instructor has to have a policy for getting that person on another team or for completing the work individually.

- Teams should have a way to divide responsibility. If someone is responsible for taking lab data and someone else is responsible for doing the analysis, the team should have a way to ensure that both jobs get done and that data are communicated. Most importantly, though, the entire team must know what went on and understand the final report.

- Teams should define how their meetings should be run. They do not need to adopt Robert's Rules of Order, but it is important to have some method of defining, for example, the chair of the meeting and rules on attendance and promptness.

Finally, some have indicated that there might be a fifth stage to team development (Tuckman and Jensen, 1977):

- *Adjourning:* When all is over and done, there should be a formal process to end the team—a lunch or dinner together, an awards banquet, a meeting in a parking lot to burn a copy of their contract. Who knows? For a well-functioning team, this is a time of some sadness, and even a short ceremony helps them gain closure.

Regular Group Processing Assessment

One essential component of cooperative learning is that groups should regularly assess their progress. If the cooperative learning group is a formal team, then it should regularly assess in what stage it is in the Tuckman model. This does not need to be a long process, but it should be done regularly.

In a regular assessment, group members should discuss the following points:

- What is working and what is not working. If they are having a difficult time setting a meeting, then they should review their agreed upon method for setting meetings. (Something should change at that point.)

- If something is working, the group should note that. There might even be improvements possible or ways of using those approaches that are working elsewhere in the project.

- There should be definite decisions made about practices to keep and practices to discard or change.

Summary

To summarize, problem-based learning is a kind of active learning and provides the same benefits that accrue from any active learning technique. It is based on problems found (conceivably or actually) in real life. Their relevance motivates students to learn what's needed to solve the problem.

PBL also has numerous cognitive benefits. One supposition we make is that PBL often puts students into different locales as they gather to work on a problem (assuming this is a group activity) and at least, gets some of the work done out of the classroom.

PBL is best implemented using group work—either collaborative or cooperative. Cooperative learning has particular characteristics that help an instructor get past some common (and well-founded) concerns. Generally, we believe that PBL is a valuable weapon in the arsenal of any instructor who wants to generate enthusiasm and produce learning that lasts.

What's Coming Up

In Chapters 5 through 8 we have given our attention to various aspects of active learning and in doing so encountered a few claims about an important topic, transfer of learning. "The purpose of formal education is transfer" (Halpern and Hakel, 2003, p. 38). Simply put, we want our students to use the knowledge they gain in our courses later in life, at different times, in different settings. They need to retain pertinent information and be able to retrieve it and apply it later in applicable situations. However, transfer is a difficult topic, and that's where we head next.

9

Transfer

What Are Your Course Outcomes?

We need to step back a bit and ask about our goals for students. We want them all to do well in our courses, to get good grades, and to do well on our quizzes and exams. But all of that really means nothing in the long run. Ultimately, we want our students to do well in life and to retain what we have taught them so they can use it wherever and whenever they need to. The problem is that if we want that to happen we should be teaching with that end view in mind. And we hope that we can somehow measure how effective we were in that effort, but we realize that measuring how well students retained material years later is not something done easily in the here and now.

In this chapter we are going to be working with the concept of transfer, which has two major aspects: (1) long-term retention of material; and (2) an ability to use and apply material in situations different from the ones in which material was learned. This is exactly what you want for your students. Transfer is the holy grail of teaching, at least in our opinion. This chapter aims to show you the importance of striving for transfer.

Transfer is often deemed to be elusive and almost impossible to achieve. There is a great deal of negativity regarding the possibility of achieving transfer, even among researchers in the general area who are often reluctant even to attempt to work in this area. Catterall (2002, p. 151) sums up this pessimism well: "Transfer has acquired a tarnished reputation over the years in the realms of learning and developmental psychology—transfer is difficult to achieve, and it is not often found, at least through the methods by which it has been studied. Under the circumstances, it is not surprising that research on transfer lay fairly dormant in recent decades. Why pound one's head against a wall in anticipation of non-publishable research findings?"

There is some evidence that the pessimism and hopelessness toward transfer is not completely warranted. For example, regarding the testing phenomenon (Chapter 6 in this volume), we found that a test asks students to retrieve information from their long-term memories and that they were better off if they practiced retrieval using free-recall tests instead of studying and trying to put more information into long-term memory. In particular, we found that practice at retrieval helped to produce better retention. The experimental work waited only a week or so to check retention, but the effect even then was significant (Karpicke and Roediger, 2007). We need to determine what other approaches we can use to improve retention.

Besides improving retention, though, we also need to worry about whether our students can actually transfer what they have learned to diverse situations. In this book, the term *transfer* often means both retention and transfer. In other words, transfer has come to include the original concept of transfer bundled with retention, as it became obvious that long-term retention was a necessary condition for transfer. But retention and transfer may not be the whole story.

Robust Learning

Robust learning has three essential elements (Pittsburgh Science of Learning Center, 2010):

1. When students learn material, they should still be able to recall and use that material after time has gone by. Students

shouldn't forget the material the day after the final exam. Teachers should aim for long-term retention by students.

2. The material students learn should not be something they can recall years later only if we put them into the same classroom where they learned the material and give them another test. We want them to be able to use the material in different situations, wherever they need that material to answer a question or solve a problem.

3. The material students learn should enable them to learn related material later. If they are going to learn basic electromagnetics in a physics course, then that should help them when they go to learn about electrical circuits in an electrical engineering course. The ability to learn related material is in addition to transfer but constitutes part of robust learning—the ability to learn related material better and faster.

Robust learning has all three of these qualities, and it differs from common definitions of transfer by the addition of a requirement that students be able to learn related material more easily.

The three aspects of robust learning are really intimately connected. If you don't have long-term retention, then you certainly won't be able to use the material. And increasing your ability to learn related material is highly desirable and should be something we aim for. Learning related material easily is probably an indication of a well-developed schema for the material and a schema that other material is easily linked to. And learning related material would seem to be an example of transferring knowledge of one topic to other, related, topics. Determining if students have retained knowledge is certainly possible, and we can also visualize how we could test for transfer. Testing whether some particular knowledge helps students learn related material is particularly difficult to determine. We are going to focus on the first two aspects in this chapter, even though the most desirable goal would be for students to achieve all three components of robust learning.

If you think about it, you don't really care if your students can do calculations sitting in a classroom taking a test. What you really care about is whether they can use the knowledge when they need to on the job. However, we can't test students in a realistic job situation, so we take their performance on a test in a classroom as an indicator of how well they will do when they need to apply the material. Unfortunately, their success on a test offers no guarantee that they will actually be able to use their knowledge if you take them out of the classroom. As we have seen, a great deal of evidence suggests that they won't be able to use their knowledge in an environment that is different from the classroom, and not much evidence points to successful transfer.

Mestre (2002, p. 4) notes that "our educational system is inefficient at teaching in ways that promote transfer. Whether measured by standardized tests, or by laboratory studies of transfer, it is evident that transfer of knowledge is elusive." Thus, be wary because transfer may be difficult to achieve even though it is a desirable goal. Transfer is something that happens later, usually in a different environment, so it isn't going to be something that you can test for at the end of a course and in the same classroom where the material was taught. If you do achieve it, you may never know. Hopefully it is not that famous "unreachable dream."

This chapter considers approaches to teaching and learning that have some promise of achieving that goal.

Working Toward Transfer

Interestingly, even though transfer is often elusive, one piece of evidence indicates that it can indeed be attained. Chapter 7 outlines how Mannes and Kintsch (1987) discovered a powerful technique based on inconsistent outlines or advance organizers. They found that students using an inconsistent outline apparently learned less initially but performed better when tested after some time had passed and that they were then able to use and apply what they had learned. That is evidence for improvement in long-term retention and for some transfer. Many writers have indicated that transfer is difficult, if not impossible, to achieve. We want to examine their claims because they do not seem to approach the problem from the viewpoint of constructing and modifying schemata. We will start by looking at how people define transfer and will examine some of the subtle distinctions that are apparent in these definitions. After we have examined that thread we will attempt to weave it back into the tapestry of earlier chapters. First, what is transfer?

> [Transfer is] the ability to extend what has been learned in one context to new contexts. (Bransford, Brown, Cocking, Donovan, and Pellegrino, 2000, p. 51)

> The underlying rationale for any kind of formal instruction is the assumption that knowledge, skills, and attitudes learned in this setting will be recalled accurately, and will be used in some other context at some time in the future. We only care about student performance in school because we believe that it predicts what students will remember and do when they are somewhere else at some other time. (Halpern and Hakel, 2003, p. 38)

Both of these references clearly indicate that the essence of transfer is that the knowledge taught and learned will eventually be applied elsewhere at another time, in another place, in another context, and that the most important thing is that students be able to use that material in those new times, places, and contexts. Halpern and Hakel (2003) embed that sentiment in a section titled "The First and Only Goal: Teach for Long-Term Retention and Transfer." In other words, performance in the classroom on a test matters only if it enables students to use the material when it really counts. If good performance on a test does not lead to long-term retention and transfer, then good performance on the test means nothing.

Let's examine what might be a very extreme example of transfer. This story just happens to be true and has an interesting side note. If it seems to take a detour, bear with us. During the World War II, torpedoes were used by the United States and Great Britain in attempts to sink German boats. Those torpedoes were not very accurate, so they were modified to incorporate a radio control signal that permitted adjustment of their course after they were launched. The Germans picked up on this fairly quickly and devised schemes to jam the control signal rendering the control useless.

Now, musicians know that a musical tone is an audio signal at a single frequency. They also know that a musical melody is a sequence of musical tones that change at prescribed times. (The artistic reader might not like this seemingly cold description of a melody, but we are engineers.) A musician suggested that the torpedo control signal could have a frequency that changed in time just like a musical melody, and that scheme was patented by two musicians, one of whom was famous actress Hedy Lamarr. It was implemented successfully and solved the control problem. This serves as an excellent counterexample for those who claim that transfer is almost impossible.

Positive and Negative Transfer

It is well known that transfer can be positive or negative. Bransford et al. (2000) present examples for mathematical tasks where people learned a simple algorithm for solving a problem and stuck with that algorithm on other problems even when simpler solutions could readily be seen by someone who had not acquired the experience that reinforced the algorithm. In other words, there is considerable evidence that people who learn a way to solve a problem using some particular method will stick with that method, even when easier methods are available.

Bransford et al. (2000) discussed a classic experiment using a sequence of "jar problems." The first problem is as follows:

> You have two jars. Jar A holds 29 ounces. Jar B holds 3 ounces. You need to obtain 20 ounces. You can pour water from one jar to another, and you can fill or empty jars if desired.

This particular example problem can be solved by doing the following:

- Empty Jar A into Jar B. This leaves 26 ounces in Jar A.

- Empty Jar B.

- Empty Jar A into Jar B. This leaves 23 ounces in Jar A.

- Empty Jar B.

- Empty Jar A into Jar B. This leaves 20 ounces in Jar A.

The experimenters used a sequence of several problems that could all be worked using this exact algorithm. After several problems, the subjects applied that algorithm to every problem, including the following one:

> You have three jars. Jar A holds 23 ounces. Jar B holds 49 ounces. Jar C holds 3 ounces. You need to obtain 20 ounces.

Here all you need to do is fill Jar A and then empty A into C—moving three ounces out of A, leaving 20 ounces in A. A "naïve" group of subjects saw that solution easily, but working a sequence of problems solvable with the original algorithm blinded the conditioned subjects to that simple solution, and they continued to use the original algorithm, which is much more complex but still works for this problem.

What has happened here is an example of negative transfer. Working the first set of problems has a negative impact on the ability to find the better solutions that exist. Negative transfer happens everywhere, and exposing students to the possibility provides a challenging metacognitive exercise for them.

Ed, who teaches electrical engineering, devised an exercise for his students. He experimented with some operational amplifier circuits in an electrical engineering course. A set of circuits could be analyzed (the output voltage could be calculated from the input voltage and circuit parameters) using two assumptions plus some general knowledge of circuit analysis to produce an accurate description of circuit behavior. Then Ed introduced a "ringer"—a circuit for which the assumptions were not valid. Students would doggedly attempt to use the invalid assumptions even in the face of experimental evidence obtained in lab that things were not working as predicted. Negative transfer effectively prevented them from working the new problem. Similar kinds of exercises could be developed with many different kinds of content, and we think that by working with them students could learn a profitable lesson.

It is interesting to reflect on what happens here. Students build a schema that works, and they prove that it works as more of these circuits are considered. The approach built into that schema works for a diverse set of situations. But students should be aware of the assumptions that are built into that schema. The one situation that is not solvable using that schema constitutes a contrasting case and a very severe contrasting case that forces students to examine the assumptions that have become built in. After students have encountered clear evidence that the schema (or schemata) will not let them handle this new problem, one of two things can happen. Either they realize that their assumptions were incorrect, or (most often) a "time for telling" arises where the instructor can engage the students, helping them out of their frustration and getting them to examine their assumptions and to realize the limitations of their approach (which they may well have come to hold very dearly and strongly).

This approach creates an excellent learning opportunity. It is, however, only a window of opportunity, and it could close quickly given how frustrated students feel. We believe that the instructor has an obligation at this point to assist students in constructing or modifying the schema. If instructors do not intervene, then this becomes an opportunity for negative transfer rather than a learning opportunity. Instructors need to intervene at the right time and with an explanation that helps students understand what has happened and why.

The learning opportunity is an opportunity for students not only to question the assumptions built into the schema first developed but also to learn how important it is to question their assumptions. That's the kind of metacognitive activity that is deemed desirable in the three key findings in How People Learn (Bransford et al., 2000), and it should be something that you want your students to learn to do. We suspect that, by questioning assumptions, students become more aware of the structure of their schemata that they have internalized. By doing this, the schemata become more easily accessed when needed—for an application, for example.

Even if you can eliminate negative transfer, you still want to build positive transfer—which would assist in further learning. How do you achieve that? We will come back to this later, but first we will continue to examine how various writers have categorized transfer in different ways.

Near and Far Transfer

Learning to drive is often used as an example of transfer. If you have learned to drive a car and your friend Ralph lends you his pickup truck, you almost certainly will be able to drive the truck, even if you have never explicitly learned to drive a pickup truck. Most people have no trouble transferring their learning in that situation. Driving a truck after you've learned how to drive a car is an example of near transfer. (Thinking back to the last section, it is also an example of positive transfer.) The new situation in this case is "near" to the learning situation you had originally experienced. (If you are thinking ahead, there is no accepted way of actually measuring distance, so near transfer and far transfer can be somewhat difficult to differentiate.) One valid conclusion gleaned from the literature is that near transfer is highly probable when the initial learning is something that becomes automatic—like driving a car (Perkins and Salomon, 1994).

Near transfer is often the goal. For example, learning to fly an airplane is easier and definitely less expensive if students can use a flight simulator. Flight simulators are used often when people are first learning to fly and when experienced pilots are introduced to new aircraft (since simulators can be designed to simulate specific kinds of aircraft). There are many other kinds of simulators; for example, they are used to train operators of nuclear (and other) power plants. Using a simulator permits students to experience situations that would be dangerous if they were operating the real system. In situations like that the goal is to make the simulator behave as much like the real system as possible. In other words, the simulator is designed so that transfer from the simulator to the real system is as near as possible.

Of course, near transfer is not always the goal. In many disciplines it is expected that students will be able to use the material later in situations that are far removed from the classroom and thus much father from the original situation. This is called far transfer, and it has an interesting history.

Even though it wasn't always called far transfer, as a basic idea it has been around for a while. The entire college educational system in the United States was based on an extreme concept of far transfer 150 years ago. At that time, most colleges assumed that training in Latin and Greek disciplined the mind and would produce graduates who could apply that discipline of mind to any undertaking whatsoever. That is an extreme example of far transfer. As time went on, the claim was investigated (Thorndike, 1924; Thorndike and Woodworth, 1901) and found to be utterly without merit. If there is any transfer effect, it is limited to faster learning of Romance languages, or the European languages that are evolutionary descendants of Latin, which is near transfer. Classically based education was a well-ingrained, but totally unfounded, educational fad. Lest you feel too smug, we wonder if the system in place today is any more well founded.

Basing an entire college education on learning the classics and classical languages is an extreme example of (hoped for) far transfer, but it's not the only example. In relatively recent years, computer programming was thought to engender general problem-solving skills. That assumption (and, again, it was an assumption with no evidence for its truth) is also not true. We might guess that the search is still on for some basic skills that transfer to a wide variety of other areas of knowledge, but they have yet to be found. Despite these educational urban legends regarding transferable skills, far transfer is not an impossible goal for teachers. Some examples of far transfer do not aim for anything nearly as extreme as the mental discipline concept.

The subtitle for this chapter is "What Are Your Course Outcomes?" The goal of our teaching should always be transfer. We don't care how well our students perform on exams and problems in a classroom, but we do care how well they can perform after they graduate. Performance in the classroom on an exam is important only if it somehow predicts how well students will be able to use that material when they need it—in life and on the job. This means that we must understand what conditions can help us teach so that transfer is achieved. What we really need to know is whether there actually are indicators we can aim for—like the ability to apply (Bloom's taxonomy—Level 4) material. Would achieving the application level in Bloom's taxonomy guarantee transfer? Would that increase the probability of transfer? Would achieving the application level have any effect at all?

If we understand transfer and realize that it is an ultimate goal of education, we next need to consider what can be done in the classroom to stimulate transfer and what we should aim for in the classroom. There are two issues here: to determine (1) what conditions might be necessary to permit transfer to happen; and (2) how to take advantage of those conditions so that transfer actually occurs when we implement those teaching–learning strategies in our courses. First, let us examine the literature regarding conditions for transfer.

Conditions for Positive Transfer

Transfer doesn't happen automatically—although many instructors seem to work on that assumption. Perkins and Salomon (1990) whimsically refer to this as "The Bo Peep Theory of Transfer": Leave them alone, and they will achieve transfer. But it doesn't happen that way.

There are at least two places in the literature where we can find sets of conditions claimed to be necessary for transfer. Bransford et al (2000, p. 53) observe the following about the conditions necessary for positive transfer:

- Initial learning is necessary for transfer, and a considerable amount is known about the kinds of learning experiences that support transfer. The prior knowledge that students bring is important. Recall the work of Schwartz and Bransford (1998), which gives an approach for generating usable prior knowledge using contrasting cases.

- Knowledge that is overly contextualized can reduce transfer, whereas abstract representations of knowledge can help promote transfer.

- Transfer is best viewed as an active, dynamic process rather than a passive end product of a particular set of learning experiences.

- All new learning involves transfer based on previous learning, which has important implications for the design of instruction that helps students learn. Generating links to other material is the most important instructional activity.

Perkins and Salomon (1994) also list conditions for transfer, some similar to and some different from those in Bransford et al. (2000). Perkins and Salomon state that when these conditions are satisfied; then transfer occurs or the amount of transfer that occurs is increased. (It does not appear that these should be viewed as necessary conditions. Rather, consider the idea that if these conditions are satisfied, then the probability of transfer is increased or the amount of transfer is increased.) Perkins and Salomon give descriptive phrases for their conditions:

- There must be thorough and diverse practice.

- Students must have explicitly abstracted critical attributes of a situation (critical abstraction).

- Students must engage in active self-monitoring.

- There must be a condition of aroused mindfulness (arousing mindfulness).

- Metaphor or analogy must be used.

We can examine these two sets of conditions and see what is common and what we can learn from the differences.

Abstraction

One common element in the two lists is the idea of abstraction. Bransford et al. (2000, p. 78) notes that "abstract representations of knowledge can help promote transfer." Perkins and Salomon (1994, p. 205) indicate that "explicit abstractions of principles from a situation foster transfer," and they give some concrete reasons for why abstraction is desirable. Schemata that are more abstract will lead to better transfer, according to both of these lists.

Learners generate internal representations or schemata of their knowledge, and those representations can be very abstract. An example here would be use of second-order linear differential equations. We have engineering students learn principles of differential equations—a very abstract form of knowledge—before we ask them to apply that material to things like damped vibrating mechanical systems (e.g., cars with springs and shock absorbers) or decaying oscillations in electrical circuits. If students have learned the principles of differential equations well, they will arrive with a very abstract representation of the concept of second-order differential equations. Then, there is an opportunity to invoke that abstraction (i.e., bring that abstract representation or schema into short-term memory) as students learn material based on that abstraction and attempt to apply it to real problems. Making that connection, or link, during processing seems to be what Perkins and Salomon (1994) are advocating, but it will not happen if the abstraction does not already exist in students' minds. Thus, Perkins and Salomon argue that abstractions should be preexistent in students' minds when starting to learn material that could be linked to those abstractions. Before going on, we should note that a great deal of mathematical concepts are, in fact, learned as abstract concepts.

In cases where abstraction has to be preexistent, programs based upon a just-in-time concept—where mathematics is presented to students only when they have reached a point in a physics course that demands a particular concept in mathematics—may be eliminating completely any possibility for preexistent mathematical abstractions. This is certainly an area for investigation. There is also a probable connection with the first condition stated in Bransford et al. (2000) that "initial learning is necessary for transfer." But stress on the importance of abstract knowledge conditions is what might be meant about initial learning. The claim here seems to be that initial learning that is abstract may be more valuable than knowledge that is not abstract. We might want to view a representation of the kind of schemata being produced like Figure 9.1.

Here, the central idea is the abstract concept, which can be applied to numerous different cases in different areas. In the process, students are building a core schema that has links to numerous different areas. That gives them practice building those links. The result is a schema that has been linked to several different areas and that should be more easily linked to new situations. We have found no support in the literature, but we suspect that the more linked a core schema is to applications the more easily it can be linked to other applications.

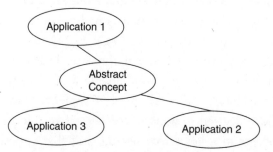

Figure 9.1 Abstract Schema Linked to Several Applications

Let us address some of the other conditions for transfer proposed in Bransford et al. (2000). First, initial learning is important: "Transfer is affected by the degree to which people learn with understanding rather than merely memorize sets of facts or follow a fixed set of procedures" (p. 55). This seems to say that learning should not be at the lower levels of Bloom's taxonomy if transfer is the goal. To get positive transfer, Bransford et al. clearly imply that you need to teach to get students above the lowest levels in Bloom's taxonomy. That might not necessarily mean a high level of abstraction even though it is a higher kind of learning. However, as we noted earlier, the ability to apply knowledge is important, which means students should at least get to the application level in Bloom's taxonomy.

If learners and teachers should work toward higher levels in Bloom's taxonomy, there is an implication that less material will be covered, simply because it takes more time to get students to the higher levels in Bloom's taxonomy. However, our watchword is "Less is more." By teaching less material and taking students to higher levels in Bloom's taxonomy, they can learn more because with good transfer they can learn more in the long run. If getting to these higher levels in Bloom's taxonomy helps transfer, then less is, indeed, more. Students can learn more because positive transfer can permit them to learn more easily any material that is related and can be linked (for a note on the importance of reducing course content, see Tobias, 1992, p. 105).

The second observation—to avoid overly contextualized knowledge—is also key. There are numerous examples of individuals unable to use information that is highly contextualized. The most extreme example in Bransford et al. (2000, p. 62) is Brazilian street children who could do the mathematical calculations necessary for street sales but who were unable to do exactly the same kinds of calculations in a school environment. Many of us see students who do well in a classroom but are unable to apply the same concepts in a laboratory setting, and that's another, albeit reverse, example of lack of transfer.

The point here seems to be that overly contextualized knowledge is more difficult to connect to when learning something related but new. We would argue that overly contextualized knowledge is probably not very abstract. In one sense, abstract material could be viewed as material that has cut ties with context and is thus applicable to different contexts. But highly contextualized material is intimately wrapped up in a single context.

The remaining observations from Bransford et al. (2000) focus on initial learning—the learning that the new learning should build on and connect to. Learning aimed at understanding is better than memorizing—implying strongly that lower levels of Bloom's taxonomy are not the goal. In addition, time on task is not desirable unless it includes deliberate practice. Also, the testing phenomenon is really good evidence that time on task is not the critical factor. Remember that it may take a long time to become an expert in an area. Finally, motivation to learn is important.

Perkins and Salomon's (1994) observations tend to focus more on conditions for making good connections when processing. For example, using analogy and metaphors can be viewed as a deliberate attempt to make connections to previously learned material. However, if you do make those connections, you also make connections to anything else for which the analogy or metaphor applies. If you use a fluid flow analogy for electrical current, for example, it takes you to other material that shares that analogy like blood flow, traffic flow, and heat flow. In the process you are most likely helping students construct a more abstract and general model that can be applied to all kinds of flow. (Finally, see the note at the end of the chapter about using analogies.) Using analogies seems to be the reverse of using abstractions and linking them to applications. Analogies that exist between different applications are really applications in search of an abstraction. The goal should be to distill the abstract representation out of the analogous applications.

Perkins and Salomon (1994) also focus on two related properties of transfer learning—active self-monitoring and aroused mindfulness—which fall into the category of metacognitive learning, or getting students to think about the process of learning, especially as it is occurring. When combined with their other recommendations, a synergistic effect should result. Using analogies while encouraging students to reflect on their use of analogy (self-monitoring) gives the kind of practice that helps students think about possible analogies when learning future material.

If the conditions discussed in this chapter are present, we still need to consider teaching strategies that will actually produce transfer. Some (e.g., use of analogy and metaphor) point directly to some specific teaching strategies, but others are not directly implied therein.

Summary

This chapter has introduced some ideas related to the topic of transfer. We have considered a definition of transfer along with various kinds of transfer, including positive and negative and near and far. We also explored some of the conditions that help transfer to occur and found that abstract representations are easier to transfer to concrete situations than the other way around. Finally, getting to the application level in Bloom's taxonomy is beneficial for transfer.

What's Coming Up

In the next chapter we will examine some suggestions for increasing the possibility of transfer.

10

Teaching for Transfer
Applying What Is Known

The present chapter will explore how to teach to produce transfer in light of the discussion in Chapter 9. As we study the literature and its recommendations, we should keep in mind that transfer is the combination of (1) long-term retention and (2) an ability to use material in situations that are different from the situation in which the material was learned.

Long-Term Retention

Some of the literature addresses how to promote long-term retention. A good starting point is Halpern and Hakel's (2002, p. 38) list of 10 recommendations, the "single most important variable" of which is "practice at retrieval." This is reminiscent of Karpicke and Roediger's (2007) finding that *repeated retrieval during learning is the key to long-term retention*. In other words, learning depends on the number of complete retrieval events, and long-term retention of the material is enhanced when students have had several retrieval events.

Long-term retention is a prerequisite for successful transfer, and if there is long-term retention then the material must have been learned in the first place. Simply put, students need to learn the material if they are expected to be able to use the material in any context. Not reckoning with that fact is at the heart of a number of failures to find transfer. As Bransford and Schwartz (1999, p. 63) note, "One important finding from research is that effective transfer requires a sufficient degree of original learning. Although this seems obvious, a number of claims about 'transfer failure' have been traced to inadequate opportunities for people to learn in the first place." We have discussed elsewhere that students get retrieval practice in many other ways, including well-designed open-ended problems, case studies, and simulations.

However, according to the literature, methods other than getting retrieval practice may yield better long-term retention. In Chapter 8 we encountered some work by Mannes and Kintsch (1987) regarding consistent and inconsistent organizers. For problem-solving activities, students who were more responsible for the construction of their schemata performed better after a delay of a few days. In other words, introducing the desirable difficulty of an inconsistent outline forces more of the responsibility for schemata construction and organization onto students, which leads to better long-term retention. We also think this evidence indicates that material will probably be retained better and that students will be able to perform at higher levels in Bloom's taxonomy when they encounter desirable difficulties as they construct and modify their schemata.

Both of these techniques focus on construction of schemata and strengthening memory traces or links to the material being learned. Also important is the kind of schemata that are constructed as well as that the end result not be a highly contextualized schema (Perkins and Salomon, 1994, Section 3).

Decontextualization

The second recommendation in Halpern and Hakel (2002, p. 39) is that "varying the conditions under which learning takes place makes learning harder for learners but results in better learning." This recommendation is aimed not at long-term retention. Instead, it is clearly aimed at the second aspect of transfer, putting the learning into situations in which the material is less contextualized and that speaks to the construction of schemata that have minimal irrelevant links.

Assume that you and your colleague Gerry have two classes of students and with the same schedule: Monday, Wednesday, and Friday at 9:00. Gerry's class meets in the Bombastic Building in Room 101, and yours meets in the Barnburner Building in Room 105. The two buildings are side by side. Would you exchange rooms with Gerry on Wednesdays for the entire semester—requiring your class to remember to go to the other room every Wednesday? Gerry's room has the same seating capacity as yours but looks very different.

This example points to how learning can easily become so contextualized that it becomes dependent on the location in which it occurs. By varying the location, the learning will become less dependent on that particular location. This might not cure all of the context-related problems, but it could be a small start. And if you teach a course that is large and your class gets split into two sections for the final, check the relative scores of the group that gets shifted out of its regular meeting room. One author had a circuits course with a relatively low enrollment. For variety of context, he met that course in the assigned room on some days and in a lab (fortunately there was a lab room with enough seats) on other days. The course lab itself was in a third room. He didn't take any measurements or do any comparisons. He did it just to put students into a variety of physical contexts. You may be able to do something similar. We also need to consider the varied way that irrelevant links can be generated in students' schemata. Every time they learn material, that material is linked in various ways to several things:

- To other material used at the same time. For example, if your students are learning about electromagnetic waves, along the way they may pick up a lot of information about gamma rays and things like early radio broadcasts, especially if you use those kinds of things as motivational material.

- To various aspects of the physical surroundings, especially if all instruction and learning occur in the same room.

Those linkages may or may not be relevant to the material. Surely links to physical aspects of the surroundings are not links that the instructor would want students to have. But even linking information about electromagnetic wave and early radio broadcasts might not be desirable. For example, there were interesting uses of electromagnetic waves in early radio and in the schemes that Nikola Tesla proposed for distribution of electrical energy. In either case, the instructor would prefer that students have a more abstract schema with more than just links to facts peculiar to the examples used.

If students have a schema like those previously discussed, we say that it is contextualized, and that kind of contextualization is not desirable. Contextualization may be unavoidable in problem-based learning (PBL), but to get an abstract representation in students' minds requires a process of decontextualization: "Unfortunately, in many real-world situations and many laboratory experiments on transfer, there is nothing to provoke the active decontextualization of knowledge" (Perkins and Salomon, 1989, p. 22).

This strongly implies that we actually need to provoke active decontextualization and not to assume that it will happen automatically. Halpern and Hakel (2003, p. 39), in their third recommendation, offer something that is particularly interesting in light of what we have noted about decontextualization: "Learning is generally enhanced when learners are required to take information that is presented in one format and 're-represent' it in an alternative format." By re-representing material in an alternative format, students are starting to remove the material from the initial context in which they learned the material. Halpern and Hakel recommend having students draw a concept map, noting that showing the network of ideas can enhance learning.

Perkins and Salomon (1989, p. 22) also note the utility of "deliberate mindful abstraction of a principle." That is what material re-representation is moving toward—an abstract representation —but it may only be a small first step in that direction. Constructing a concept map can help students form a more abstract representation or schema, with all references to context removed, insofar as that is possible.

These considerations and recommendations lead us to conclude that a strong requirement for transfer is that the instructor should put learners in situations that encourage construction of more abstract schemata.

Some Further Ways to Decontextualize Material

Students do not construct abstract representations automatically. We need to consider what we can do that will put students in situations where that outcome has a better chance of happening. One technique we have encountered is "contrasting cases" (Schwartz and Bransford, 1998, p. 475), in which "analyzing contrasting cases can help learners generate the differentiated knowledge structures that enable them to understand a text deeply." The goal with this method is to get students to construct "differentiated knowledge structures" (i.e., schemata). This approach gets students to focus on the differences in cases but also to extract the common features in superficially different cases. It's not clear if that always produces an abstract schema in students' minds, but it does seem to be a step in that direction.

For example, temperate and tropical rain forests provide two cases of *rain forests*. The differences and similarities between a temperate rain forest (in, e.g., northwest Washington State) and a tropical rain forest (in, e.g., the Amazon or New Guinea) can be contrasted, analyzed, and used to aid in student understanding of the concept of a rain forest. Regarding river deltas, the deltas of the Nile River and the Mississippi River can be used as contrasting cases of river deltas and river delta formation. There are also numerous examples to demonstrate flow rate and pressure interdependence—where a change in one flow path alters conditions so that flow in other paths is changed simultaneously. For example, if you are in the shower when someone else turns on another shower, the temperature of your water changes, sometimes dramatically. In electrical current flow rate, an automobile's lights may dim when you turn on the starter. More examples can be found in the areas of electrical current flow and sewage flow. The point is that trying to get more or less flow changes the driving force (e.g., pressure, voltage) that causes the flow in the first place.

Contrasting cases share a common, abstract model that can be applied to the situation. The instructor should devise a problem or question that explicitly asks students to develop an abstract model starting from multiple concrete instances (two is probably sufficient) that exemplify the model, which requires students either to resolve the differences or recognize them as irrelevant to the general model. The net result is a more abstract model that can be used to make predictions in different situations involving particular instances of the general, abstract model.

The method of contrasting cases is something that the instructor can use to help students decontextualize material. But do be careful; if you run out of time and can't get to the second case, you might find that students who have learned a concept in the context of a particular problem might have a difficult time remembering and accessing that material in a different context. Using a single problem may prompt students to generate highly contextualized schemata. It is the resolution of differences that forces students to sort out any essential, core elements of a concept and to strip away the details of the context. What remains should share common elements—the essence of the abstract model they should be aiming for. Now is the time to explicitly ask students about those commonalities.

Contrasting cases are an excellent method to help students develop more abstract models and improve chances of transfer. They also seem to fit the idea of active decontextualization, since considering contrasting cases that arise in different contexts would tend to blur the context dependency of each individual case.

Halpern and Hakel (2003, p. 39) recommend that material be re-represented. This is an interesting recommendation because it does not involve two or more instances of a concept that you want students to abstract. Rather, when students are asked to generate two different representations for a body of material, they must notice where the differences between the two representations must be resolved. An activity that uses the idea of re-representation follows:

- Construct an outline for the material. Be sure that each main topic has related subtopics included in a bulleted list.

- Construct a concept map for the material.

  - Then, show how the concept map and the outline are related—noting similarities and differences, or have different concept maps critiqued by different groups in the class.

If students are asked to construct both the outline and the concept map, they will have given you two different representations of the knowledge structures they have generated in their minds for the material they are learning. That is what Halpern and Hakel (2003) are suggesting students do when they recommend re-representing the material.

To review, in building knowledge structures that support transfer, (1) practice at retrieval improves long-term retention; and (2) some form of active decontextualization helps to generate a more abstract knowledge structure.

Other approaches have also been suggested to support transfer. Shank (2004, p. 3) notes that for transfer a good strategy is to "intentionally extract underlying principles. . . . For transfer situations where the learner is expected to apply skills in diverse situations, they need to be able to recognize and then apply underlying principles. Instruction can intentionally determine how similar elements are used in very different contexts."

The reference to underlying principles is really a reference to a more abstract knowledge representation. Notice that the recommendation is to "intentionally extract underlying principles," which means that students will have been working on a specific problem first and that the underlying principles must be extracted from that example. This is different from the method used in contrasting cases where students are asked to give two or more examples in different contexts and then extract the underlying principles or "decontextualize" the schemata that have been produced.

Bransford and Schwartz (1999, p. 64) note that "concrete examples can enhance initial learning because they can be elaborated and help students appreciate the relevance of new information. However, despite its benefits for initial learning, overly contextualized information can impede transfer because information is too tied to its initial context. Presenting information in multiple contexts can increase subsequent transfer." The conclusion here is that you might want to use PBL to help students learn, but if students encounter only one problem in a very specific context, that material will be tightly bound to that context; you will need to use at least one other problem in a different context and then help them extract the principles from those two different contexts. In effect, you will be using contrasting cases, but the timing will be different from what was investigated by Bransford and Schwartz (1999, p. 504) because you will be introducing the contrasting case in a second problem that comes later—not concurrently with the first problem.

Now that the Pandora's box of PBL has been opened, there is an interesting observation that we'd like to make. Many of the books about PBL advocate that students be given a particular methodology for PBL; what follows is a generic version:

1. Encounter the problem.

2. Define the problem.

3. Propose several solutions to the problem.

4. Evaluate the proposed solutions and choose one.

5. Flesh out the details of the solution.

6. Evaluate how well the solution actually works.

7. Go back to Steps 3 and 4 if the solution does not work well enough, and repeat steps after that.

8. Implement the solution.

9. Evaluate the implementation.

In this approach, the students are being given a problem-solving schema the instructor thinks will work for them. We should expect that this approach will probably not work as well as the instructor wants. Can you see why?

Now consider an alternative approach:

1. Give the students a problem to solve.

2. Let the students solve the problem. Do not require that they follow any particular problem-solving method, but give guidance and advice as necessary.

3. Give the students a second problem to solve that might be related to the first in that it requires retrieval of the same concepts or material.

4. After the two problems have been solved, have students abstract their own set of rules for solving those problems by reflecting on what they did when they were solving the two problems. Comparing and discussing different problem-solving prescriptions is a good technique to process the results of this exercise.

The two problems that they solve constitute a set of contrasting cases, and if you are doing a good job they will probably have a few more cases to reflect on as you go further in the course. This approach makes students responsible for construction of their own personal schema for problem solving, and we know full well that they will not remember a schema that they are simply given.

Is Decontextualization Always Necessary?

There will be times when decontextualization may not be necessary because the material was learned in an abstract (i.e., context-free) format to begin with. Mathematics concepts are necessary in engineering and science and are usually taught in separate mathematics courses by faculty that teach only mathematics. In those courses, often few, if any, applications are used to illustrate the material.

If we teach in a discipline that uses mathematics, we often bemoan this fact. The question is whether that is actually detrimental to the students. Bassok and Holyoak (1989, p. 154) examine the "ability to apply mathematical procedures" to problems that are "structurally isomorphic." In other words, the mathematics problems and the physics problems use the same underlying abstract knowledge structure. The authors point out, "Training in algebraic equations for solving arithmetic-progression problems, coupled with exposure to example word problems, allowed robust transfer to unfamiliar but isomorphic constant-acceleration problems in physics . . . In contrast to the robust transfer observed from algebra to physics, the results obtained with physics students in Experiment

1 indicated that transfer between the two isomorphic domains is strikingly asymmetrical. Students who had learned how to solve constant-acceleration problems in a physics course gave no indication that they recognized any similarity between such problems and arithmetic-progression problems with nonphysics content" (p. 154).

These results show why abstract representations of knowledge are so important. An abstract representation of mathematical concepts learned as algebra was able to be transferred to a physics course, whereas the same mathematical concepts learned in a physics course—and embedded in the context of a physical situation —did not transfer to the algebra course. In a way this says that we are doing something right when we send our students off to the mathematics department to learn that material. If we take a just-in-time approach we would need to be very careful that students actually built abstract representations of their mathematical knowledge. If they do not build those abstract knowledge structures, then the risk is that everything they learn in that situation becomes highly context bound and, consequently, unusable in other contexts—unless, of course, there is an active process for decontextualization.

There is other evidence indicating that abstract representations lead to better transfer. Sloutsky, Kaminski, and Heckler (2005) describe overly contextualized learning situations as having "irrelevant concreteness"—that is, concreteness that gets in the way of development of more abstract representations.

> The fact that irrelevant concreteness was found to hinder both learning and transfer may have important implications for our understanding of learning of complex domains, specifically that of mathematics and science. The dominant view in the educational community has been that perceptually rich, concrete, and entertaining materials are useful for acquisition of

knowledge and transfer of this knowledge outside the learned situations. Our research suggests that although intuitively appealing, this view may be very limited. In order to facilitate learning, perceptually rich, concrete representations must communicate relevant aspects of the to-be-learned information. However, even then there might be a tradeoff between learning and transfer. In addition, the results of the present research indirectly suggest that learning of mathematics, which is populated by abstract entities represented by generic symbols, can facilitate learning of science, which is populated by more perceptually rich, concrete entities. (p. 513)

The quote phrases this claim in a particularly compelling way, and reading the entire paper is worthwhile. In a way, use of "perceptually rich, concrete, and entertaining materials" is, as Sloutsky et al. note, "intuitively appealing." But there are times when our instinct to make our educational materials more appealing is something that we have to hold in check. Simple, abstract representations, although less entertaining, are what help the most to facilitate later learning.

Some Other Observations

We have presented a case that practice at retrieval and active decontextualization can help effect transfer, but other variables should be considered as well. Schroth (1997, p. 71) claims that reducing the frequency of feedback to learners can increase transfer: "Among the major findings was that although lowering the percentage of feedback trials slows concept attainment, it facilitated transfer on all transfer tasks. In general, the fewer the number of feedback trials subjects received, the greater the amount of transfer. The results are consistent with other studies that suggest that conditions that make it more difficult for subjects to initially learn a task may have positive benefits for transfer."

This strongly implies that using "desirable difficulties" is a way to facilitate transfer. Desirable difficulties put learners in situations where they need to take more responsibility for construction of their schemata, and we noted earlier that this produces richer schemata, with more and stronger links to other knowledge structures. Desirable difficulties seem to be a pedagogical version of the old adage, "No pain, no gain."

Hugging and Bridging

The presumed difficulty of obtaining transfer (according to much of the literature) has led to a strong suggestion that transfer might be achievable if the learning situation is extremely close to the situation in which the learning will be used. That is the thinking, for example, behind building simulators for systems like power plant control rooms and aircraft. This concept is called "hugging" because the learning situation is made to be as close as possible to the application situation—that is, the learning situation "hugs" the application situation. Perkins and Salomon (1994, p. 6456) refer to hugging as the "low road to transfer." Hugging "recommends that instruction directly engage the learners in approximations to the performances desired. For example, a teacher might give students trial exams rather than just talking about exam technique, or a job counselor might engage students in simulated interviews rather than just talking about good interview conduct. The learning experience thus 'hugs' the target performance, maximizing likelihood later of automatic low road transfer." Using hugging is an attempt to make the student performance automatic —just as driving a car or reading is automatic. When the behavior is automatic it is more likely to come forth in a real application situation.

Hugging is not difficult to implement in engineering or science courses. For example, you can place problems in the context of an imaginary company. Then, you can create various roles within the company and maybe convince fellow faculty members to play those roles. Author Bill has a film of author Ed acting very curmudgeonly as he attempts to get a class of chemical engineers to design a pump. Films like these can be reused.

However, by using hugging it almost seems like giving up. If we make the learning situation identical to the application situation, then the material being learned surely will be highly context bound even though the closeness to the application will increase motivation. In addition, the material being learned might be used in that one application situation and nowhere else. An educational experience like that is very useful when that one application must be learned well, but if students' entire educational experience consists of hugging experiences, they might not adapt well to new situations and may not be particularly inventive and productive of new applications.

Bridging is somewhat the opposite of hugging and is sometimes referred to as the high road to transfer. Perkins and Salomon (1994, p. 6456) say, "In bridging, the instruction encourages the formulation of abstractions, searches for possible connections, mindfulness, and metacognition." Thus, bridging is pretty much what we discussed earlier in the chapter, particularly with the emphasis on abstractions. Perkins and Salomon seem to add an aspect of student reflection on what transpires as they are learning (mindfulness and metacognition). And we might particularly want to reflect on that aspect of abstraction as we consider the next section on analogies.

Using Analogies

As far back as the ancient Greeks, people have been advocating the use of analogies as a powerful tool in helping students' understanding. For example, when students first encounter a model of a hydrogen atom, they are often asked to think of it as a miniature solar system with a proton at the center, like the sun, and an electron revolving around it, like a planet (e.g., Earth).

Analogies are often used on intelligence tests and college admission tests:

- A finger is to a hand like a toe is to a _____?
  (Fill in the blank.)

- A:B::C:?

In these examples, it is not completely clear what kinds of representations we have, but something in the representations of fingers and hands lets students infer what the missing element is. The given pair (finger: hand) is called the source, and the target is the pair with an unknown element that must be established.

In most instances where we want to use analogy in the classroom, we assume that students already possess knowledge that forms the source. For example, if they know that a difference in water pressure causes water to flow, the following scenario might be plausible to them:

> Assume that you have two cities, City A and City B. For a long time there has been no net movement in population between them. Now City A has attracted some new companies with highly desirable jobs, and with those companies now building their new facilities, City A has embarked on projects to improve its school and park systems. In addition, in anticipation of those developments various entrepreneurs have begun opening new entertainment facilities, for example. City A now has a desirability rating increase and the difference in desirability will cause population flow.

- In which direction will population flow? From A to B, or from B to A? If the flow decreases to half of the initial flow after 3 years, what do you infer about the difference in desirability between the two cities?

- If you think in terms of a water flow analogy, what are the variables (a) population flow and (b) desirability difference analogous to?

The real question, however, is what happens here? Aristotle viewed analogy as two situations with a shared abstraction. This gets pretty much to the heart of the matter, and remember that an abstraction is also another representation of the same concept. We believe that if you do not work with students to get them to understand that abstraction, then you have lost an opportunity for deeper learning.

Although they are often difficult to create, analogies are advocated, for example, in Bransford, Brown, Cocking, Donovan, and Pellegrino (2000, p. 66), who indicate that "successful analogical transfer leads to the induction of a general scheme for the solved problems that can be applied to subsequent problems. Note that general scheme underscores the sentiment of getting students to understand the shared abstraction. Fogarty, Perkins, and Barell (1992) provide a list of 10 tips for teaching for transfer.

However, using analogies can be difficult because students are not apt to notice when one exists, which means that it will not be easy for them to discern the shared abstraction. For example, Bransford et al. (2000, p. 64) discusses a general who must capture a fortress located in the center of a country with many roads radiating out from the fortress. The roads are mined, which limits their "troop-carrying" capacity. The solution is to split troops into smaller units so that they can travel many roads to the fortress without exploding the mines. After students are given this problem, an analogous situation is shared in medicine in which a doctor wants to deliver a lethal dose of radiation to a tumor. Delivering the radiation along one path will kill all of the intervening tissue (a radiation carrying-capacity limitation), but by using several paths to the tumor a lethal dose can be delivered to the tumor without killing all of the intervening tissues. The authors note, "Few college students were able to solve this problem when left to their own devices. However, over 90 percent were able to solve the tumor problem when they were explicitly told to use information about the general and the fortress to help them" (p. 52).

Students may well have analogical information that can help them, and once connections are made (i.e., when the shared abstraction is found), the information leads directly to a solution. However, students may need to have someone point out the connection. Using analogies can be effective, but the teacher should expect to do a lot of coaching because it's unrealistic to expect students to be able to figure out on their own where an analogy works. Trying to get students to make connections using analogies and metaphors can be frustrating. The root of this lies in knowing that students "own" a knowledge structure that matches what they need but that they are unable to use the knowledge you know they have. It also behooves us to realize that this happens often. You can help students discover the shared abstraction by asking them explicitly what the shared features of the two situations are and to state their results in general (i.e., more abstract) terms. Overall, analogy can be a useful tool, despite its limitations and challenges, which we suspect occur because it is difficult to extract the shared abstraction.

Before we leave this topic, we always need to be cognizant that no analogy is perfect. Earlier we mentioned the Earth–sun analogy for the electron–proton model of the hydrogen atom. However, the earth can be any size, and every electron is identical; in addition, the earth's orbit could conceivably vary slightly, but the possible orbits for an electron are fixed. Those facets of the analogy are incorrect if they are applied to the hydrogen atom. Every analogy has some aspects that do not transfer; if they are transferred in students' minds, we're back to the problem of negative transfer.

Forrest Gump said, "Life is like a box of chocolates. You never know what you're going to get." This is an apt analogy for analogies. Not only do analogies serve as connections between the source and the target and the underlying shared abstraction. Also, Gentner (2002, p. 28) catalogs six ways they can lead to "knowledge change," which we interpret as changes in students' knowledge structures or schemata.

Gentner (2002, p. 28) points out that analogies permit "highlighting and schema abstraction—extracting common systems from representations, thereby promoting the disembedding of subtle and possibly important commonalities." Disembedding is interpreted as another way of saying decontextualization, so this refers to developing more abstract schemata. She also says that analogies permit "projection of candidate inferences from one domain to the other" (p. 28). That is, what you can infer from the source might also be "projected" as an inference for the target.

In addition, analogies allow students to notice "alignable differences —becoming aware of contrasts on dimensions or predicates that are present in both analogs and/or that are connected to the common structure" (Gentner, 2002, p. 28). Thus, features in the target might be inferred from features in the source, and students might not have thought of that otherwise. To achieve this you might have to prod students to think consciously of all the features in the source and ask them to determine if those features are present in the target. Analogies also help in "re-representation— altering one or both representations so as to improve the match (and thereby, as an important side effect, promoting representational uniformity)" (p. 28). In the course of using an analogy, the mental representations of the source and the target tend to become similar, possibly changing both of students' mental representations.

Analogies also permit "incremental analogizing: extending the mapping by returning to the base domain for more material to add to the analogy" (Gentner, 2002, p. 28). In this case, the analogy would be built incrementally as students notice more features in the source that might carry over to the target. Analogies also allow for "re-structuring—altering the domain structure of one domain in terms of the other" (p. 28.), which seems to be a case of taking incremental analogizing to a higher scale, possibly restructuring both source and target representations (schemata) in a wholesale way as a result of using the analogy.Keep these possibilities in mind, as well as how analogies can provide links to other schemata.

Summary

In this chapter we discussed several ways to increase chances for transfer. To transfer material, students need to learn it in the first place—they cannot transfer what they don't know. In addition, the material should be known at higher levels in Bloom's taxonomy than memorization or comprehension (the two lowest levels). Learning the material that way facilitates long-term retention, and transfer is impossible if students do not retain the material.

To promote transfer, decontextualize the material. Have students re-represent material in a different format. This implies that students have developed some sort of abstract representation of the material.

Use feedback judiciously. Students need to construct their own knowledge structures. Trying to give them your knowledge structures will lead to them memorizing your input and not constructing the kinds of schemata they need.

Finally, use bridging and hugging as well as analogies and shared abstractions as appropriate.

What's Coming Up

The next chapter will draw material together from the entire book with the goal of solidifying the approaches that are most reasonable to use in the classroom.

11

Applications

This chapter offers suggestions for how to use the material in this book. We are not going to give you recipes that point to particular techniques. Rather, we are going to examine some particular points in the teaching process and try to point out what is important. That way you can apply the concepts from the book in a way that will let you evaluate methods that you encounter— whether it is something you find in the literature or a suggestion from a colleague. The most important thing to take from this book is an understanding of what is important in the learning process, and we will examine ideas from that perspective.

If you want to become a good teacher, first of all, be yourself; don't do something because it seems to work for a colleague. Rather, be sensitive enough to see if it works for you. Everyone is different, and what works well for someone else may not work for you. In addition, move slowly. It is probably not a good idea to try to read through this book and immediately attempt to adopt every suggestion. Again, if you get an idea, examine and evaluate it within the context of the learning process as we have presented it. If it seems to be well founded, then you can try to use it in class, evaluate its effectiveness, and keep it in your toolbox and move on to another technique. This chapter suggests things to try as you begin.

As we go through the chapter we will develop a set of questions that you can ask as you encounter ideas to incorporate into your teaching. These questions will try to put ideas into a framework consistent with the model presented in the book.

Some Reflections

Understanding how students learn is one thing, but as a teacher you still have to figure out how to apply that knowledge in the classroom to help your students to learn better.

To get to that point, a frequent objection must be addressed; for our purposes, we will use an analogy with an engineering situation. Imagine that you are a mechanical engineer designing a vehicle of some sort. Obviously, if you are working on a vehicle that moves, Newton's laws of motion apply:

1. An object at rest will remain at rest unless acted on by an unbalanced force. An object in motion continues in motion with the same speed and in the same direction unless acted upon by an unbalanced force.

2. Acceleration is produced when a force acts on a mass. The greater the mass (of the object being accelerated) the greater the amount of force needed (to accelerate the object).

3. For every action there is an equal and opposite reaction.

These three laws have served us well since their inception. Interestingly, though, they often run counter to everyday observations. For example, if you roll a ball on a flat floor, it will eventually stop and not continue in motion with the same speed. We all know that from the floor there is friction, which is a force acting on the mass to slow it down. In fact, the first law refers to an ideal situation that exists only in the vacuum of space far from any gravitational field or "unbalanced forces." Only by first considering idealized situations and developing abstract laws are we ultimately able to get to the point where we can apply those laws in complicated situations far from the ideal, like designing a vehicle.

When we have approached faculty about using some of the concepts in the literature in the classroom, they often object on the principle that some of the research was not done in a classroom where we propose it be used. It is true that actual classrooms include complicating factors that may not have been taken into consideration when doing the research; however, if the description of the learning process is accurate then this research should not dismissed. What takes place in students' minds is what is important, and the research gives insight just as Newton's laws apply to situations in the world—situations that are far from the ideal situations where those laws were initially posed.

These objections puzzle us, frankly. We three authors have engineering degrees, and in our experience it is unusual to find a body of knowledge in physics or chemistry that we had not mined for anything applicable. Indeed, scientists, particularly physicists and chemists, communicate with each other and with the engineering community—not always perfectly but well enough that it doesn't take long for new conceptual knowledge, say, the wave nature of the electron, to find its way into the design of the electron microscope or for the theory of relativity and radioactivity to find its way into nuclear power plants, nuclear medicine, and atomic bombs. In science and engineering, if there is conceptual knowledge available, engineers and scientists cooperate and communicate to use that knowledge in the design of devices. What is known about learning should similarly be applied in the classroom and the design of educational experiences. It should not be taking so long for this to start to happening. Research like what we've highlighted in this book can be applied in classrooms, so in this chapter we would like to specifically explain how you can use the concepts encountered throughout this book to produce better learning in the classroom. We will reexamine the learning process, and as we go we will summarize what we have discussed as being effective. At the end of the chapter we provide some personal advice taken from our experience in applying active learning.

Some Things to Consider

You may be tempted to do a complete redesign of all of your courses to incorporate the ideas from this book. While that may be noble, it might take more energy and time than you have. As an analogy, consider the difficulty of getting a totally electric car for sale and on the road. You may know the goal, but the path from start to finish is filled with potholes. The biggest difficulty in applying technological research results centers on the kind of person you are. If you have been teaching for a while, you have accumulated a variety of teaching techniques that over the years you have become comfortable with. Even if you are fresh out of graduate school, your entire experience may involve teaching based on a transmission model—not a constructivist model. Thus, you may well feel uncomfortable trying to implement some of the ideas contained in this book. You need to learn what you are comfortable with, so your first task is to "know thyself." In other words, you should probably start simple and go in stages; as you become more comfortable you can implement more ideas.

The next section reviews the learning sequence and then identifies the kinds of things that can be implemented at different points in the learning sequence. You may discover some things with which you are comfortable and others you might at least initially prefer to forgo. We don't recommend that you go through this list sequentially and start working on the first thing you find. Read this material in its entirety, and then make a conscious, deliberate decision on where you want to start. Along the way we will identify ideas we think make good starting points for those who haven't tried this before. We will start at the beginning and follow through the learning process.

Working Through the Learning Sequence

To review, in the learning process you first need to evaluate what students bring to the table to determine what their preconceptions and misconceptions might be. Then you need to help students get rid of any misconceptions they bring with them. A word of warning: This is probably the most difficult step in this sequence. Next, students need to encounter the material they need to learn. You might present the material or have students read textual material or encounter the material online. After this, students need to process the material (1) to build schemata that are more like those of experts through schemata-building activities; and (2) to strengthen links between old and new schemata, possibly through retrieval practice. Finally, you need to evaluate how far students get in this process. Actually, you may need to do this at all the stages of this process.

That's a fairly typical sequence of events in terms of what happens compared with what we really want to happen. That will allow us to link that with concepts from earlier chapters.

Addressing Misconceptions

What Do Students Bring?

Earlier we encountered examples of learners who started with an incorrect knowledge base, such as that the world was round and coming to "know" that the world was pancake shaped, combining their new learning (i.e., that the world was round) with their previous "knowledge" (i.e., that the world was flat). The story of the fish and frog also drove that point home. The lesson to take from examples like these is that the instructor needs to know something about what knowledge structures the students possesses when they enroll in a course.

This can be a discouraging step in the process. If students were in a memorization mode in their prerequisite courses, you may find that they have retained little or nothing. There is a story about a professor who was discouraged because this always happened to her, and she resolved to teach the prerequisite course herself so that her students in the follow-on course would be adequately prepared. She gave it her best, only to discover that her students were no better prepared than they had been when others taught the prerequisite course. Her teaching generated good student evaluations, and she was confident that she taught well—just like those who had previously taught the prerequisite course. So be prepared to discover that students have serious misconceptions and to determine what they are if you can, even if you are confident initially that no such misconceptions exist.

Uncovering Misconceptions

Before you start to present material, remember that students arrive with some knowledge of the subject, which could be a preconception or a complete misconception. Bransford, Brown, Cocking, Donovan, and Pellegrino (2000) give three key findings. The first one concerns the preconceptions and misconceptions students bring with them: "Students come to the classroom with preconceptions about how the world works. If their initial understanding is not engaged, they may fail to grasp the new concepts and information that are taught, or they may learn them for purposes of a test but revert to their preconceptions outside the classroom" (p. 14).

In a companion volume, Donovan, Bransford, and Pellegrino (1999) give several recommendations about misconceptions and preconceptions, including the following:

- "Teachers must draw out and work with the pre-existing understandings that students bring with them" (p. 15).

- Teachers must identify and address "preconceptions by field" (p. 42).

- Conduct research on preconceptions of teachers regarding the process of learning (p. 48).

Thus, it seems clear that you must uncover student misconceptions, but how do you go about discovering what they believe and think?

First, you can give precourse exams or quizzes to determine what students do and do not know. You should probably expect that students will not perform as well on your exams or quizzes as they did at the conclusion of the course (or courses) where they learned the material. After all, some time has elapsed since they learned the material, and many elements of the context have changed including the room, the student cohort, and probably the instructor, all of which can affect typical quiz and exam performance. You also have to consider that typical exams and quizzes are good retrieval opportunities—even if they emphasize material at the lowest level in Bloom's taxonomy—so that you can actually use your preliminary exam or quiz as a learning event. Let's be even more specific about these exams and quizzes.

More specifically, you could give students a short test on the material they should know coming into your course. Don't use a multiple-choice test; it's not a good retrieval event, and the teasers on them can lead to learning the teasers instead of what you want them to know. Instead, you could use a short-answer test, because it might help students learn the material better. In addition, a short-answer test can give you information about misconceptions —especially those that might be shared by many of the students. So you should try to use a test that allows students to generate their own answers.

Once the misconceptions are identified, try to do something about them. You might have a debate with some students presenting and defending the misconceptions and others presenting and defending the other side. This is not a waste of valuable class time. The real waste of time is proceeding as though nothing is wrong only to find out later—say, at the end of your course—that students still hold tightly to those misconceptions they brought with them to class. If you are teaching in an area in which a concept inventory is available, you can use the concept inventory to uncover student knowledge of the course area, and to help identify misconceptions. Concept inventories (Halloun and Hestenes, 1985a) are not currently available in all areas, but they are well worth using if you can get one.

A second way to see where students are is to ask them to explain, either verbally or written, the material that you want them to know coming in. Either way provides an opportunity for retrieval, but in this case it is at the second level in Bloom's taxonomy. The short-answer test asks students to perform at the lowest level in Bloom's taxonomy, so this gets one level higher.

A third way to determine where students are is to ask them to apply the concepts you are concerned about in a realistic problem. You may well be asking for some serious transfer when you do that since the context is considerably different from the context in which the material was learned. Remember that this will be a retrieval opportunity at an even higher level in Bloom's taxonomy— the application level. This puts the onus on you to generate appropriate problems, which could take some time, especially the first time you use this technique in a course. Keep all the problems you use as well as ideas about other possible problems because you may need them the second time through the course. And share them with others teaching in the same area; they might have some ideas you can use.

One other method we think has considerable merit is asking students to draw a concept map for the material (Turns, Atman, and Adams, 2000), which can be generated quickly and gives a picture (literally) of the schema (or schemata) for the material of interest. We're not suggesting you grade these concept maps. You need to interpret them, somehow evaluating the concepts that are linked in students' minds and the richness of those links. Ultimately, you need to judge how well students' concept maps match what you would expect from an expert in the area. Evaluating student concept maps takes more time than grading a single-answer test. However, you aren't going to get much useful information from a single-answer test, and the information you get from student concept maps can give a really good picture of the state of their knowledge. It is particularly useful to have students prepare a concept map when you first introduce a topic and then a second map once the material has been covered and hopefully learned.

Davis (1997, p. 34) recommends "introduc[ing] a topic and then ask[ing] a question which brings out their knowledge such as 'What's going on here? How do we know that?' If student answers are recorded, the same questions can be posed again at the end of the topic or term to evaluate students' progress." Asking questions like this helps you to determine not only what students know, including knowing misconceptions, but also whether they can explain what they know with any depth.

Montfort, Brown, and Findley (2007) recommend using individual interviews, which could take considerably more time. Still, as they point out, there is "substantial evidence" that students graduate still in possession of initial misconceptions (Chi and Roscoe, 2002). An education that does not rid students of misconceptions is hardly effective.

Generally, we think that these methods will give a good idea of where students are when they enter your course. Our list is not exhaustive. This is an area where considerable work is being done, so it might be a good idea to do a Web search for what is available. The best advice is to take advantage of every opportunity to let students expose how they know what they know. These techniques are all very deliberate attempts to expose misconceptions. Bear in mind that you won't learn much about students' misconceptions if you give them true–false or multiple-choice quizzes. Give them a chance to tell you about their knowledge so you can identify misconceptions and move on to helping them to get rid of them.

At the end you should ask yourself, "Do you have a better idea of what student misconceptions students bring to your course?"

If you can answer that question positively, you will probably want to start developing an inventory of common misconceptions so that you can use that information the next time you teach the course.

Correcting Misconceptions

Once the misconceptions are identified, they need to be corrected, which is more difficult than identifying them. Substantial work has been done on the persistence of misconceptions (Chi and Roscoe, 2002; Nissani, 1997). Festinger, Riecken, and Schachter (1956) offer a compelling description of how strongly some individuals will hold onto misconceptions even in the presence of strongly disconfirming evidence (e.g., spaceships arriving to pick up those who would be saved and taken into space to join the extraterrestrials). History is replete with examples where overwhelming evidence disconfirms some new concept—whether it involved the end of days or the phlogiston theory—with true believers continuing to cling to their mistaken beliefs. Misconceptions can, at times, have amazing staying power. Kuhn (1962, p. 151) quotes a morose Planck as saying, "A new scientific truth does not triumph by convincing its opponents and making them see the light, but rather because its opponents eventually die, and a new generation grows up that is familiar with it." (That's enough to make you pessimistic, isn't it?) Changing misconceptions in students has been likened to changing paradigms in science (Kalman, Morris, Cotlin, and Gordon, 1999), so don't expect it to be easy.

To help students get rid of misconceptions, you first help them identify the misconceptions. Students must be *aware* of the misconception and must be *dissatisfied* with the misconception. This implies that you must put students into a position where the misconception fails when they use it to predict some event—and it is probably desirable that a failure to predict correctly carries a grade penalty. Science, technology, engineering, and mathematics

(STEM) disciplines probably would use some sort of experiment or experience highlighting the discrepancy, which in turn forces students to face the disconfirming evidence. Students may well invent an alternative explanation for the failure for any particular case. (Remember, when the spaceship doesn't come to pick you up, you can decide you got the time and date wrong.) As we have said before, it's not going to be easy. You need to supply students with the correct explanation, which is necessary but still not sufficient. "Supply" means an explanation is available—telling will definitely not work in this situation. You also need to help students build a better schema incorporating the correct explanation. Problem-solving work puts students into situations where they have to defend their misconceptions. Arguing with someone who has a better schema is one good way to force a student to confront, and hopefully correct, misconceptions.

Because correcting misconceptions is not an easy task, here are few other suggestions that might help:

- Well-written simulators for the subject material (if you have access) can help expose students to consequences of misconceptions. Then having them make predictions in varied situations can help produce improvement.

- Laboratory work helps. Mother Nature has a propensity for pointing out misconceptions by producing disastrous laboratory results.

- Try in-class demonstrations with group work after a demonstration so that students have to interact with other students who have a variety of schemata.

Eric Mazur (1996), a physics professor at Harvard University, was shocked by the results of a test on Newtonian mechanics he gave to his students. The results indicated they had only memorized equations and were unable to use the material even in the simplest kinds of applications. He decided to switch to what he calls peer instruction. At the beginning of class, he gives a short quiz on the assigned readings. This motivates students to read the material so that they are prepared when they come to class. Then the lecture part of the period is broken into 10–15 minute snippets.

At the conclusion of each snippet, he gives a short concept test that requires "qualitative rather than quantitative answers." Mazur's (1996) book gives exhaustive examples of physics concept tests. This particular aspect of Mazur's book is very valuable because it gives insight into how to construct similar concept tests for other areas. Students get a minute to work on an answer, record it, and estimate their level of confidence in their answer. After that minute students have to turn to their peers and convince them of their answer. Then he surveys the class to get the new answers and a revised confidence level. He moves on to the next topic only when he is sure of students' mastery of the concept.

There are several very interesting aspects of this approach. Mazur (1996) begins with a retrieval event. Then, breaking the class into 10- to 15-minute snippets is one way to ensure that working memory never gets severely overloaded—if it gets over-loaded at all. We will have more to say about that in the next section on perception. The concept tests put students in a position of dealing with their conceptions and can help them to realize that they might be misconceptions. These concept tests happen fre-quently through a period, and to us that seems like repeatedly hitting on a rock with a hammer. Sooner or later the rock breaks, and sooner or later students see that they have a concept that is actually a misconception. Developing answers to questions and having to present them to their peers and then defend their con-cepts is a very good method for students to construct and recon-struct schemata. Finally, he moves on only when he is fairly sure that most students are with him.

Davis (1997, p. 30) notes that concept maps can be used to help students correct misconceptions: "Students constructing concept maps in cooperative groups show a greater increase in conceptual learning than students working individually, thus the utility of concept mapping may depend on the instructional setting." We suspect that puts the students into a situation where they have to defend linkages between subtopics, and concept maps can help students to identify misconceptions and also to correct misconceptions. "Cooperative group work on concept-focused tasks had a significant effect in helping college students overcome certain misconceptions in chemistry, even though it did not involve concept maps." Finally, Davis (1997) provides some ways to help correct misconceptions. Among them are first to anticipate common misconceptions. Be alert for other misconceptions. You will have to assess the concepts held by students often. Look for resources that identify common misconceptions in your area. There is active interest in identifying common misconceptions, and an Internet search could prove valuable. Second, put students into situations that test their conceptual frameworks. Use discussion with other students. (You may want to listen in to those discussions.) Have them think about the evidence and possible tests of the concepts. Third, devise or find demonstrations and lab work that address common (and other) misconceptions. Finally, work on common misconceptions as often as you can.

It also seems pretty clear that if you follow this advice you will have to take more time with your students. Davis (1997, p. 30) notes that "helping students to reconstruct their conceptual framework is a difficult task, and it necessarily takes time away from other activities." We believe that it's absolutely necessary, though. If you don't find and address students' misconceptions, you undermine all of your other efforts. At the end of this you will need to ask yourself, "How do I know that initial misconceptions are now corrected?" You will probably need to measure where the students are at this point.

Perception

As you wander around a college campus today, you often see semi-darkened rooms, projectors aglow, and someone in the front (or back) of the room blissfully reading PowerPoint slides to students barely awake. Forgetting that these electronic drones put vast numbers of students into a groggy state, the question remains about what happens to those who manage to stay awake.

A typical electronic slide presentation is very highly organized—and we will have more to say about organization much later. We can learn what kind of organization is in a typical presentation of that sort by examining some of the kinds of suggestions given to users of those presentation programs:

- Limit what you put on a slide. For example, one heading and three bullet points may be the maximum you should put on a slide. Be wary of any slide with more than 25 words.

- Give an outline and follow it. (Mannes and Kintsch, 1987, just might disagree with this one.)

- Make each slide a discrete idea.

The common advice is to limit the amount of material on any one slide if you want the slide to be effective. After all, each slide has a limited amount of space, and you need to use a large enough font to be read, for example, in the back of the room. We think you ought to start by questioning what it is you are teaching if it can be presented in small little chunks like that. Is that the way the material really ought to be organized? Is that the way students should organize the material in their minds? Inquiring minds want to know, because there surely is material that consists of many highly integrated and connected pieces that should be stored in long-term memory as something other than artificially small chunks.

These software presentation programs force the user to cut up the material into little chunks—often without well-defined links between them. This invites students to store things in very small, disconnected chunks. If this occurs, learners could have difficulties when they want to integrate the material another time. We call this "malchunkification"—a word we just invented but that is pretty descriptive of the problems that could result. Sweller and Chandler (1994, p. 185) present a disturbing idea: "A limited working memory makes it difficult to assimilate multiple elements of information simultaneously. Under conditions where multiple elements of information interact, they must be assimilated simultaneously. As a consequence, a heavy cognitive load is imposed when dealing with material that has a high level of element interactivity." These authors are claiming that the instructor might be teaching material where there are many interconnected elements that cannot be simultaneously present in short-term memory (working memory) because of the inherent limitations of short-term memory. (The reference to "heavy cognitive load" is taken to mean an overload of short-term memory in this situation.) They also point out that the instructor could well organize material in a way that produces a high level of interaction between the elements of the material and do that in a way that overloads short-term memory. The high amount of interactive material that overloads short-term memory could be intrinsic to the material, but it might also be caused by the way the instructor presents and organizes the material: "We are forced to process elements simultaneously when they interact and cannot be considered in isolation. Elements may interact either because of the intrinsic structure of the information or because of the manner in which it is presented or both. The intrinsic structure of information is unalterable, but, if elements interact and impose an extraneous cognitive load solely because of instructional design, restructuring is called for" (p. 226).

Electronic slide presentations impose a structure on material that might not really be present in the material. There is a strong implication from Sweller and Chandler's work (1994) that, to learn material effectively, all of the interacting material needs to be present simultaneously in short-term memory. If you break material into smaller chunks just to satisfy requirements for presentation software, you will need to be especially wary that you do not introduce extraneous information that produces cognitive overload. So what should you do? Well, you need to break your material into manageable units, teach them separately, and then later combine them.

Hopefully, you will not often have to teach material that is so inherently difficult, and you can concentrate on being effective. Here are some simple recommendations (from Chapter 4) that can be implemented fairly easily:

- Don't fill up a period with lecture or presentation.

- When you think students' short-term memories are getting full, stop presenting material, and start to process what you have presented. Help students link the newly presented material by giving them a problem that requires them to use related material with what has been just presented.

- Don't interrupt the flow until you are ready to start processing. Material out of the flow, like motivational stories, should be presented first and not in the middle of the flow of the presentation.

- Don't obsess about content. It is better to do less and do it well than to "cover" everything and have the students learn next to nothing.

- Check what students have actually perceived.

All of these recommendations are based on the fact that working memory has limited capacity and that students should process the material when their working memory capacity is reached. Of course, this model assumes a presentation by the instructor, and it doesn't have to be that way. If you were teaching in the English department—working your way through a play by William Shakespeare, for example—you would require students to read the play and any relevant background material and then would use class time primarily for processing. Why not do that in STEM courses? Here's a proposal for how to do that:

- Assign reading material some time prior to the class where it will be used—perhaps the preceding class period or at the beginning of the course on a calendar included in the syllabus.

- When students arrive in class, give them a short conceptual question to answer from the assigned readings. You can then have groups of students work from individual answers to a group answer.

- Survey groups (remembering to be sure to give everyone in those groups an opportunity to respond as the course goes along. This will help to ensure that they take responsibility).

- Repeat through the period as necessary.

These steps bear a remarkable similarity to Mazur's (1996) approach, as noted in an earlier section. In short:

- Students come to class having read the material.

- A short question gives them a retrieval opportunity, which strengthens the link to the material and simultaneously brings that material into working memory.

- They process the material by working individually and then defending their answer to their peers—a good schema (re)construction activity.

Mazur's (1996) work is persuasive because almost all of what he has to say comes directly from the classroom. We started this chapter with a note about faculty reluctance to import research results into the classroom. It should be encouraging to see someone who has, in effect, put those results into practice and who has reported on that to good effect.

Some of the activities proposed in this section are really processing activities. Even though we have already started the topic of processing, we will focus on it primarily in the next section.

At the end of your presentations, you always need to ask, "Did I overload short-term memory in the students?" If you find that you did, you will surely have to change your presentation for the next time.

Processing

Retrieval-Based Processing

Retrieval-based processing can be implemented easily and takes only a few minutes using Felder's (2003) suggestions. Retrieval events are important ways to promote learning and long-term retention. We discussed one-minute papers in an earlier chapter and noted how they give students an opportunity for retrieval. Giving a short quiz not only can be a retrieval event but also can provide some motivation for students. However, you don't have to grade every quiz that you give, and you don't even have to announce them. You can also just make it a practice to give one regularly but to grade only some of them.

This section provides a summary of a few retrieval activities. We recommend that all of these should be closed-book activities. Open-book exercises defeat the purpose of trying for retrieval events. And, in all cases, we assume that since you are trying to produce retrieval these short exercises are not done when the material is still resident in students' memories. You could defer these activities until the next class, or you could use the first 15 or 20 minutes for a topic—possibly doing some processing—and then move on to something else. Later in the class you could come back to the original topic and give these kinds of activities to the students:

- Ask the students to write a concise summary of the material that was presented earlier in the class or in the previous class (one-minute paper).

- Ask the students to write an exam question for the topic.

- Ask the students to write the single, most confusing point related to the topic. Note that there will be times when the act of determining the most confusing point clarifies the point for students.

- Have students, perhaps in groups of two or three, prepare a short (one-minute) presentation on one of the points covered. They could select from a list of topics. Interacting with other students takes these activities from retrieval activities to possible schema-building events. Sometimes it is difficult to separate retrieval events from schema-building, but it doesn't matter since the ultimate schemata that are constructed are the important things anyway.

- Spacing class time spent on a topic—by spreading it out over more class periods—provides more opportunities for retrieval (spacing effect).

- Multiple-choice tests and questions are often counterproductive.

You can do other things to give students retrieval practice. In Chapter 7 we suggested asking students questions to discover what they understand about material covered previously. In addition to probing students' knowledge, this strategy will also uncover misconceptions that you can then deal with directly. Additionally, we described two desirable difficulties that are basically opportunities for retrieval events, both of which have strong classroom implications: (1) distribute or space study and practice (don't cram; short study periods spaced out over periods of days are better than one large cramming session); and (2) use tests (rather than presentations) as learning events.

Distributing study and practice implies that students learn better if you space out material. For example, if you are teaching topic A, to be followed by topics B and C, you don't have to finish topic A before going on to the other two topics. You can try working on topic A for about 15 minutes, then going on to topic B for the same time, and finishing with topic C. The three topics might not be running completely concurrently, and A may be finished before B, but that distributes or spaces the study and practice and gives many more retrieval events.

To accomplish this, you need the cooperation of the students. They have to read the material before class, and they may need some incentive. Sacks (1996) makes it clear that getting students to read is difficult and that they always want to work toward a test. So you need something to motivate students to read; unfortunately, it will probably have to be grade based, which means you may need to grade much of the work your students do.

As you think about this, you should realize that you are starting to invert the presentation-processing way of doing things. In the typical course situation, presentations occur in class and processing occurs out of class. You are asking them to reverse where presentation and processing occurs.

Finally, we note that all of the recommendations in this section are easy to implement. If you have presented material and you think that students' short-term memories are near saturation, you can, for example, ask students to summarize what you have just presented, paraphrase what you presented in language appropriate for a high school student (or some other well-defined audience), or write an exam question for the material just presented. These activities all take the material you presented and ask students to do something with it—to think about the material in at least a slightly different way. You are taking them to the point where they are beginning to construct or modify schemata, and you are doing it in a way that can easily be inserted into a conventional class.

You need to ask some questions about techniques such as those discussed in this section. The first question is, "If I was aiming for practice at retrieval, did I achieve it?" It is all too easy to give in to student requests such as for open-book quizzes that would stand in the way of actually giving them a true retrieval event. The second question is, "Did I take advantage of the retrieval to move on to helping students to link the material with other, previously learned, material?"

Schemata-Construction Processing

The other kind of processing is based on schemata construction rather than on retrieval (although there are clearly cases, as discussed already, in the gray area between those two possibilities). Earlier in this book we discussed several different kinds of schemata-construction activities, all of which have been researched in classroom-like settings or actual classrooms:

- Reciprocal teaching (Palincsar and Brown, 1984)

- The method of contrasting cases (Schwartz and Bransford, 1998)

- Contextual interference (Mannes and Kintsch, 1987)

In these three methods, students are put in a position where they have to resolve differences in two (or more) different situations. In reciprocal teaching, students have to resolve the differences between their conceptions (or misconceptions) and the concepts held by their reciprocal teaching partner. As they debate and discuss with their partner, they must retrieve information they know (an act of retrieval). As they debate, they need to form arguments and give examples. Both of these activities create and strengthen links to other material they know, enriching the schema at hand.

In the method of contrasting cases, students have to resolve the differences between the two cases. In the process of resolution of two contrasting cases, they will have an opportunity to create a more abstract schema because they will have to extract the general principles involved.

In the contextual interference situation, students have to resolve the differences between an advance organizer that contains the same information as the presentation, but with a different apparent internal organization. In that process, students also have an opportunity to create a more abstract schema much as in the method of contrasting cases. And, perhaps, the organization of the presentation and the organization of the advance organizer are, in fact, contrasting cases.

Once you step back from these methods you might be able to think of them as contrasting cases of schema construction. The point is that you need to put your students into situations where they have to resolve differences, and you don't have to stick with the format of any of these three examples. You could give students a few related problems that involve the same principles but that look different superficially. Or you could have students create homework or exam questions deliberately designed to use the same principles in different situations, in effect asking them to create their own contrasting cases. You may even find that you get some exam questions that are appropriate, and you may well decide to use them.

There are several important things to consider in these types of activities:

- Did I give students an opportunity to defend their concepts by putting them in a position to have to defend their ideas—that is, to argue for their ideas with their peers and to evaluate the ideas of their peers?

- Did I give students an opportunity to compare different ways to apply the concept?

- Did I give students an opportunity to link concepts with previously learned concepts?

Some Reflections

These recommendations for retrieval-based processing and schemata-building processing basically turn out to be recommendations for some widely advocated kinds of active learning. However, realizing what you are trying to do can inform what you do and can increase your effectiveness.

Some activities seem to be retrieval opportunities but turn out not to be. Asking for a summary of what has just been presented might be only a dump of what is in working memory rather than a retrieval of material from long-term memory. You need to let enough time elapse if you are aiming for practice at retrieval. Timing is everything here. That doesn't mean that you should forget about activities after a presentation. Even an activity that, on the surface, seems to be a retrieval event might be a good time for a schemata-building processing event. For example, if you have spent 10 minutes presenting a concept, you could ask students to re-represent the concept or to outline the concept (assuming you haven't passed out an outline). It is probably best, at that time, to have students interact with each other. Interactivity puts students into situations where they have to organize their thoughts and present and defend them and that is conducive to building richer schemata.

As a rule of thumb, it's best to wait for working memory to clear (the next class period) if you want students to have a retrieval event. In that situation, you would probably want them to work individually. If you wanted students to have a retrieval event, did you set up conditions so that it occurred? Conversely, after a presentation, you probably want students to do things in a group setting to gain the benefits of creating richer schemata. You should be able to evaluate what happens in those different situations by reasoning from the memory model we have used throughout the book.

And Then There's Transfer

In Chapter 10 we examined some techniques recommended in the literature, including the following:

- To transfer material, students need to learn it in the first place.

- The material should be learned in a way that facilitates long-term retention.

- To promote transfer, decontextualize the material.

- Have students re-represent material in a different format.

- Use feedback judiciously.

- Use bridging and hugging as appropriate.

- Use analogies.

All of these points have implications for the classroom.

For material to transfer, students need to learn it in the first place—ridding themselves of misconceptions and forming schemata that are appropriate. However, to get long-term retention probably requires getting to higher levels in Bloom's taxonomy. That is a strong argument against any strategy that involves memorization. If students can pass your course simply by memorizing the material, they will forget that material fairly quickly—quite possibly before your course actually ends. So whenever you ask students to do something, like a one-minute paper or a simple retrieval event, you need to ask them to do so at a higher level in Bloom's taxonomy.

Next, as possible, help students decontextualize the material. Get them to encounter the material in different contexts. Not only must students work in different physical locations—to reduce the effect of place knowledge—but they also must encounter the material in different problem contexts. We believe that two good "story" problems with different story settings are better than a half dozen of the typical textbook exercises. (There is disagreement among the authors here because there is sentiment to make that several dozen instead of a half dozen.)

Teaching for transfer works best when it revolves around activities that give students practice at retrieval and activities at higher levels in Bloom's taxonomy. In particular, follow the suggestions outlined herein to help students decontextualize the material so they can build more abstract representations of the material. You could ask students to outline the material and also to make a concept map and then compare the two for each individual (e.g., hugging, bridging, analogy). Use of analogy is particular useful for schema abstraction. If you have an analogy for the material you are presenting, you can do things with it. One good thing to do is to give them the barest sketch of the analogy and ask your students to fill it in giving you points that work and points in the analogy that do not work. For example, if you are teaching electrical current, the analogy might be fluid flow, for which there are similarities (e.g., fluid being conserved at a point where a pipe diverges into two pipes) and differences (e.g., current flowing inside the material of the wire, not in an open space inside a pipe).

Collaborative Learning

Group learning experiences are at the heart of many of the activities you want students to do. Group learning puts students in many different kinds of situations where they have to defend their ideas in a way that promotes goals of building schemata and practice at retrieval. In Chapter 8 we discussed some of the things you can do to incorporate cooperative learning—like developing teams and the various techniques that help you incorporate the five tenets of cooperative learning. But don't underestimate how much students can learn from and with each other. We suggest that you do an Internet search on "cooperative learning" to see some of the rich literature available on the topic.

Our Final Reflections

As we come to the end of this book we'd like to revisit what needs to change in our classrooms. First, lectures and electronic slide presentations often fail to get students involved in ways that promote learning. There is little opportunity for practice at retrieval and for activities that help students to construct rich, expert-like schemata. But we want our students to become experts and to access what they know when they need it. To do that, we have to provide them with experiences that develop these dimensions of learning. We must work to restructure what takes place in the classroom to provide those experiences.

Well thought out active learning experiences can and should provide students with the experiences they need, but active learning experiences that provide practice at retrieval and help them actually construct their own schemata take more time than lecturing. You won't cover as much material, But students will retain what they learn and be able to use it.

Cautionary Tales and Other Advice

In this book we have shared a number of classroom approaches that can be used in STEM classrooms. A substantial amount of research supports each of them. We hope that the research along with our advice on how to implement these approaches will motivate you to adopt them. If you are considering doing so, we have some final recommendations.

First, you may want to go slowly when applying the ideas from this book. It isn't that the recommendations are wrong. However, if you haven't ever used any sort of active learning approaches, you may not be prepared for student reactions. You also want to have a plan for what you're going to do in case things don't go as planned. So, take it easy and get accustomed to teaching with active learning techniques as you go along. As you start to incorporate these ideas into your courses you will develop techniques that are uniquely yours.

If you are already using active learning methods, you may have found some things in this book to help you use them more effectively. In addition, you may have found some other things that permit you to identify methods you are using that either make little sense or that don't achieve your goals. In those cases, we recommend the following:

- Try different techniques one by one—not all at once. However, if you are already comfortable with a technique (because you have already been using it), add something new to your repertoire.

- Communicate with your students so that they know
  what you are trying to do. Give them links to the
  research findings that support and explain what you are
  doing.

Some Final Words

Authors Ed and Bill have a long history of teaching and were
convinced they were doing well using traditional lecture methods.
However, both were ultimately dissatisfied with student performance and consequently introduced numerous kinds of active
learning into their classes. Those methods were, in large measure,
based on the approaches advocated in this book. Both are much
happier with the results obtained by adding more student activity—
heads-on activity—into their classes. Getting to the point where
students accept a nontraditional classroom approach takes time,
but it is well worth the effort.

Ultimately, you cannot give anything to students except an
opportunity for them to create their own knowledge structures.
However, when you give them that opportunity, you may hear
this criticism: "That professor didn't teach me anything. I had
to learn it all by myself." That's actually a compliment, and hopefully when your department head reads a comment like that he or
she will realize you are doing what effective teachers need to be
doing.

Mazur is one person who has adopted an approach that, in
practice at least, is very similar to what we advocate. On the
back cover of his book *Peer Instruction* (1996) is a quote from
one of his students: "If you get to solve it for yourself, you are doing
the thinking. There is an 'aha!' kind of sensation: 'I've figured
it out!'—it's not that someone just told it to me, I actually
figured it out. And because I can figure it out now, that means
I can figure it out on the exam, I can figure it out for the rest of
my life."

This quote expresses a very different student attitude from the usual student complaint about instructors not teaching students anything, leaving the students to learn it on their own. If your students say something like this quote from Mazur, they have indeed learned something more important than your course content.

We wish you all the best in using the ideas in this book, and we hope that you can give this gift to your students.

Appendix

Bloom's Taxonomy and Educational Outcomes
The McBeath Action Verbs

You can take two different approaches when designing a course. You can design the process for the learning experience, assuming that a good teaching approach will guarantee that the students will learn what you want them to learn. Alternatively, you can set up specific learning objectives—skills that you want the students to acquire—and try to determine whether they are actually acquiring them. The latter is a sort of feedback approach where you have certain goals and can measure how well you are achieving those goals as you proceed.

When you are designing a course and trying to determine the outcomes you want the students to achieve, it is almost always beneficial to think in terms of the level in Bloom's taxonomy where you want the students to perform. If you are a biology professor, would you be satisfied if your students could list all of the different kinds of vertebrates? Or would you want them to be able to use the different characteristics to classify something (and it doesn't have to be a platypus)? However, if you want students to memorize (e.g., be able to recite a list of all the members of a phylum), you are specifying that you want them to be able to perform at the lowest level (knowledge) in Bloom's taxonomy; if you want them to be able to apply what they know, then you are asking that the students be able to function at the application level in Bloom's taxonomy. In other words, one way to give a clear indication of what you want the students to accomplish is to

specify the level in Bloom's taxonomy that they should reach—
what the student should be able to do—at the conclusion of your
course.

Bloom's taxonomy can be used to write very specific course
outcomes. You need to consider the following:

- You will need a verb to describe what you want the
  students to do. In the following examples, the verbs
  are italicized:
  - Be able *to apply* psychological concepts to
    contemporary issues.
  - Be able *to predict* the effect of varying environmental
    temperature on an organism's cellular respiration.
  - Be able *to calculate* the efficiency of a centrifugal
    pump.
- You should avoid verbs that lead to unmeasurable
  requirements. For example:
  - Understand the sociological perspective.
  - Understand Kirchhoff's Current Law.
  - Have an appreciation of the principle of
    Conservation of Energy.

The issue is not that you don't want students to understand the
concepts in your course; it's that you can't really measure understanding because you can't really get inside students' heads well
enough to do that. Instead, you only can ask students to do something that would give evidence of some knowledge (at some level
on Bloom's taxonomy) of the subject. The first set of examples
requires the students to do something—to apply a concept or to
predict or to calculate. When you measure the students' knowledge
(e.g., give an exam, grade a lab report), you look at what the students do. Therefore, you defer on the idea of understanding and

aim for the students to be able to do some specific things. For example, you could determine if they can apply the course concepts to situations where those concepts are appropriate or if they can recite the concepts.

Measurement now consists of putting students in situations where they have to apply or recite the appropriate concept—this is your choice if you are the person who determines what the course outcomes should be—and assessing how well they do whatever it is that you ask them to do. Outcomes for given material can be written differently for different levels of Bloom's taxonomy. Next we consider some examples of typical course outcomes drawn from different disciplines. Course outcomes for a biology professor teaching about animals' body temperature can take various forms depending on his goals. For example, a student should:

- Be able to state what is meant by endotherm and ectotherm

- Be able to explain what is meant by endotherm and ectotherm

- Be able to identify (classify) organisms as endotherms or ectotherms

- Be able to interpret data as they relate to the effect of varying environmental temperature on an organism's body temperature

- Be able to design an experiment to test the effect of varying environmental temperature on an organism's body temperature

These outcomes all address the same material but require students to work at different levels in Bloom's taxonomy.

In the same way, course outcomes for a professor teaching introductory mechanics can vary depending on her goals. For example, a student should:

- Be able to state what a free body diagram is (Level 1)

- Be able to explain free body diagrams (Level 2)

- Be able to apply free body diagrams to a structural member specified by the instructor (Level 3)

- Be able to use free body diagrams to analyze a structure (Level 4)

- Be able to use free body diagrams to design a structure for some purpose (Level 5)

Clearly, each of these outcomes require students to learn the material—whatever it is—to a different level in Bloom's taxonomy.

The outcomes from these two disciplines share the following characteristics:

- Each element of the two sets of outcomes addresses the same material as the other outcomes in the same set.

- Each of the outcomes in each set requires students to learn the material to a different level in Bloom's taxonomy.

- Each of the outcomes uses a different verb to describe what students should be able to do when they have completed the learning module.

The verbs you use are probably the most important part of writing your outcomes, and at different levels in Bloom's taxonomy the verbs you use will be different.

When you begin to write outcomes, consider first what level you want students to achieve. Beginning courses might have many outcomes at the lower levels. However, there is some evidence that aiming for (and achieving) the lower levels in Bloom's taxonomy leaves the knowledge acquired by the students in an "inert" form.

Aiming for higher levels will probably produce greater retention. Giving students hands-on experience through design and project courses permits them to function at the highest levels of Bloom's taxonomy. Courses may repeat material if later courses take the material to a higher level in Bloom's taxonomy. (The chef on TV would say, "Kick it up a notch.") If the knowledge at the lower levels becomes "inert," you may be tempted to reteach.

The goal of this Appendix is to help you write one or two outcomes for a course that you teach. Consider the level that you want your students to achieve in Bloom's taxonomy, and write an outcome appropriate for the level you have chosen. First, determine the level you want, and then write one or more outcomes. Don't fuss and fidget about what you write because this is only a first draft; you will have a chance later to revise.

As you write and revise, it is important to keep the following in mind. The verbs you use to describe what you want the students to do are important. In addition, there are some words you might not ever want to use because what you are describing might not be measurable. For example, wanting students to understand something is laudable but probably not measurable.

It isn't always easy to write usable outcomes, but you can use the McBeath action verbs to help in writing outcomes. Consider writing outcomes for the lowest level in Bloom's taxonomy (the knowledge level). Verbs that are appropriate for this level include *arrange, define, describe, duplicate, identify, label, list, match, memorize, name, order, outline, recognize, relate, recall, repeat, reproduce, select* and *state*. (These verbs are presented in Besterfield-Sacre et al., 2000.) As you look at these verbs you should be able to see that doing any of the actions described does not require the student to do anything beyond recalling material. The student doesn't have to use the material in any particular way.

If you want to write outcomes for the next higher level—comprehension—you would use verbs like *classify, convert, defend, describe, discuss, distinguish, estimate, explain, express, extend, generalize, give examples, identify, indicate, infer, locate, paraphrase, predict, recognize, rewrite, report, restate, review, select, summarize,* and *translate.* This second set of verbs asks the student to do some simple tasks that involve a little more mental effort than just reciting material (and *reciting* is a verb that could be on the first list, couldn't it?).

Similarly, Besterfield-Sacre et al. point out that we can have the following verbs at the higher level.

At the application level: *apply, change, choose, compute, demonstrate, discover, dramatize, employ, illustrate, interpret, manipulate, modify, operate, practice, predict, prepare, produce, relate schedule, show, sketch, solve, use,* and *write.*

At the analysis level: *analyze, appraise, breakdown, calculate, categorize, compare, contrast, criticize, diagram, differentiate, discriminate, distinguish, examine, experiment, identify, illustrate, infer, model, outline, point out, question, relate, select, separate, subdivide* and *test.*

At the synthesis level: *arrange, assemble, categorize, collect, combine, comply, compose, construct, create, design, develop, devise, explain, formulate, generate, plan, prepare, propose, rearrange, reconstruct, relate, reorganize, revise, rewrite, set up, summarize, synthesize, tell* and *write.*

At the evaluation level: *appraise, argue, assess, attach, choose, compare, conclude, contrast, defend, describe, discriminate, estimate, valuate, explain, judge, justify, interpret, relate, predict, rate, select, summarize, support* and *value.*

Having good course outcomes is not an end in itself. There are several things you can do with your outcomes that will help make your course go better. For example, share them with your students. Remember, you and the students should be working toward the same goals, so they really need to know what your desired outcomes are—thus defining educational goals for the course. In addition, if your course outcomes include everything you are trying to accomplish, then they also become a study guide for students:

STUDENT: Professor, what is on the final? We covered an awful lot in this course, and I don't have the foggiest idea of what to study.

PROFESSOR: I will ask you to be able to do the things listed in the course outcomes. There isn't anything else, and the outcomes were published from the first day of class. Any other questions?

You can also use your list of course outcomes when making up exams. A wise strategy is to have every exam question address a single course outcome. If you record the grades for each question separately, you will have a measure of how well each outcome was achieved. It's a little bit more work, but it gets you valuable accreditation (ABET if you're teaching engineers) data for a small price.

At the end of the course, you can survey students on their perception of how well you achieved your outcomes.

Course Outcomes

Using the concepts of Bloom's taxonomy, you can begin to write outcomes for your courses that specify what you want the students to be able to do upon completion of the course. Before you actually start writing course outcomes the following aspects should be noted.

First, outcomes should be *specific*. They will specify the level of learning expected of the students and the conditions for the learning expected, including prior information and time to achieve the learning. Key in this requirement is the time limitations on performance of the outcome. However, conditions other than time can also come into play, including the information that is necessary for achieving the outcome. A typical outcome written with this condition in mind will say something like, "Given information X and Y and condition Z, the student should be able to do 'W' in an hour."

Second, outcomes should be *achievable*. This means that there is sufficient time to achieve them and that students have the background necessary to achieve them. If your students haven't learned differential equations, you probably don't want to have an outcome that requires them to solve differential equations to achieve your specified outcome. In other words, the outcomes should not require so much that it is impossible for the average student in the class to be able to perform the outcome.

Finally, outcomes should be *measurable*. It is relatively easy to write outcomes that simply cannot be measured, the most common of which that the student "understand" (or "be aware of" or "appreciate") a concept. Understanding is some aspect of the mind, but there is no clear way to measure it. Even defining *understanding* can be difficult. Students, for example, often complain that they understood the concepts but that they just couldn't do the problems that the instructor asked them to do. Surely you want your students to understand the material in a course, but you can't really tell when they do. Consider the following example course outcomes:

In this course students will increase their understanding of the following areas:

- Problem definition and solution methodologies
- Basic electrical quantities, including charge, current, voltage, and resistance
- Electrical laws applied to real circuits
- Integral calculus applied to resistance capacitance circuits
- Kirchhoff's laws applied to real electrical circuits, including resistor combinations, voltage dividers, and bridge circuits.

The question is just how you would measure whether a student had achieved these outcomes. For the most part, these outcomes do not address the levels in Bloom's taxonomy and don't ask for specific actions on the part of the student. Remember that the main phrase concerns only understanding of the concepts listed in the bullets, but outcomes must be measurable. So, as you start to design the educational experience, you need to keep in mind one of the last phases of that experience—how you will measure your level of achievement.

Knowledge Representations Depend on the Level in Bloom's Taxonomy

We can make some interesting correlations with Bloom's taxonomy related to what we know about knowledge representations (i.e., schemata). At the lowest level of Bloom's taxonomy, students memorize the material they are learning in numerous ways. Some examples of techniques to help students memorize items on a list are as follows:

- Students can generate nonsense sentences that have the same first letter as the items on a list to memorize. For example, the sentence "Kings Conquer Actively Although Serfs Endure" can be used to memorize the levels in Bloom's taxonomy (knowledge, comprehension, application, analysis, synthesis, evaluation).

- Students can memorize a path they traverse frequently and attach items on the list to points on the path. If you traverse a path from your home to school that includes the sequence, driveway, road, stop sign, gas station, stoplight, entrance, you can attach *knowledge* to the driveway (possibly by imagining the word *knowledge* written on the driveway), *comprehension* by imagining comprehending the road, and so on. You may want to create images that—to you—give the meaning of the word, and, in your mind, put those images at those critical points on your path. When you are done, you remember the list by imagining that you are traversing the path and remembering the items attached to each point on the path. This is sometimes referred to as the method of loci.

• You have to wonder what the student did—the student we discussed in an earlier chapter who memorized the material for Friday. That student could well have encountered one of these methods in help sessions designed to aid high school students in getting better grades. (We say high school because we don't want to believe that it could happen in "higher" education.)

We're not quite sure what kind of knowledge structure is retained in your long-term memory when you use these kinds of techniques. Surely the student retains some very odd links to the material that seem to be totally useless when it comes to applying the items on the list in any situation where they are needed. What does seem clear is that the knowledge structure—the schema—generated with this method has some links that are probably best described as useless (for later application) and frivolous and that may well interfere with later serious learning related to the material being memorized. Using the method of loci is a good way to help you memorize a speech, for example, because it will help you make your points in the order you want. However, if you are in a physics course, which is very conceptually oriented, and you memorize material using the method of loci then you will most likely have extreme difficulty using that material when you need to apply it. The method of loci is excellent when you need to repeat something verbatim, but it is not a good method for learning conceptual material.

Higher levels of Bloom's taxonomy are not totally immune from these kinds of effects. You might want to consider what being able to explain a concept might mean, to some students. They might be able to memorize an explanation (from their book, course notes, whatever) and recite it when called upon. You can tell if a student is at a given level of comprehension only if that student can defend the explanation when asked.

Higher levels in Bloom's taxonomy seem to require more sophisticated knowledge structures. For example, if students are able to perform at the application level, then they have knowledge of procedures—ways to use the knowledge—in their schemata. At this point it is also safe to assume that the students have links to other knowledge and schemata since they are able to apply the knowledge being learned to appropriate situations. It is our belief that being able to perform at higher levels in Bloom's taxonomy is a good indication that students possess more complex schemata relating to the knowledge being learned. (Determining if more complex schemata indicate an ability to perform at higher Bloom levels would be a possible research topic. To this point we have not found any published work done in that area.) Thus, getting students to move to higher levels in Bloom's taxonomy helps them create more complex and usable schemata. There is a chicken-and-egg question here. Do more complex schemata help students apply knowledge being learned, or does practice at application help create those more complex schemata? Either way, a reasonable goal for many courses would be to get students to the application level.

If we want students at the application level, we need to have a clear idea of exactly what we want them to achieve. We can express this by writing clear outcomes for our course using McBeath action verbs and by specifying the level in Bloom's taxonomy that we want the students to reach—the application level, at least. With a clear goal in mind, we need to consider teaching and learning strategies that will allow us and our students to achieve our goals.

Glossary

Abstraction: The process of removing concrete properties from a concept to produce a concept not tied to a specific problem. *See also* Decontextualization.

Active learning: Any activity that requires learners to construct their own knowledge.

Advance organizer: An outline of material to be learned that is given to students prior to the learning event.

Bloom's taxonomy: A way of characterizing levels of knowledge.

Bridging: The process of establishing connections between initial learning and seemly unrelated other situations.

Chunking: The process of mentally grouping items that are related.

Clustering: A way to begin writing by using a process of grouping ideas. Related to concept maps.

Collaborative learning: Learning in groups.

Complete retrieval: A retrieval event that comes after material is completely flushed from working memory.

Concept maps: A method to elicit a visual representation of schemata.

Contextual interference: A cognitive dissonance introduced by two different, seemly inconsistent versions of the same material.

Contextual problem: A problem embedded in a situation that gives meaning to the learner.

Contrasting cases: Two examples illustrating the same concept in a way that requires students to resolve apparent differences.

Cooperative Learning: Collaborative learning with the specific conditions stated in the five tenets of cooperative learning.

Decontextualization: The process of removing material related to a specific event to establish a generalization. *See* Abstraction.

Desirable difficulties: A way to have students overcome inconsistencies in learning difficulties introduced during initial learning in a way that reduces initial performance but enhances long-term retention.

False memory: A condition in the mind in which incorrect meaning is stored that appears true to the learner.

Far transfer: Transfer to a situation that is different from the original learning, such as, transferring the concept of a musical melody to a frequency-hopping method in communication.

Gist memory: A section of memory where the understanding or meaning of specific learning is stored.

Graphic organizer: A method that presents a concept in a visual form.

Hugging: An attempt to produce transfer between closely related situations. *See* Near transfer.

Interactive engagement: An activity that requires learners to mentally create and apply schemata.

Kolb cycle: A sequence of four types of activities that is claimed to give students in each Kolb learning type an opportunity to use their preferred learning style.

Long-term memory (LTM): A location where knowledge that is permanently learned is stored. *See* STM.

Mozart effect: The (unproven) theory that students learn better by listening to certain types of music as they learn.

Near transfer: Transfer to a situation that is very similar to the original learning, such as from driving a car to driving a truck. *See also* Hugging.

Negative transfer: Transfer that impedes the use of material in different situations.

One-minute paper: An active learning technique in which students summarize their current learning in a few brief statements.

Positive transfer: Transfer that enhances the use of material in different situations.

Problem-based learning: An active learning technique where a problem drives the learning.

Processing: Integrating newly acquired material with what learners already know.

Reciprocal teaching: An active learning technique that involves a student in the role of a teacher of other students.

Retrieval: The act of moving a knowledge structure or a part of a knowledge structure from long-term memory to short-term memory.

Retrieval event: A process of bringing information from long-term memory to working memory (short-term memory).

Robust learning: The result of methods that produce long-term retention, transfer, and preparation for future learning (PFL).

Schemata: A mental structure that organizes information, processes, and concepts.

Short-term memory (STM): A location where newly perceived information is temporarily stored. Material from long-term memory can also be moved temporarily into STM. *See* LTM.

Spaced retrieval: Achieved by having students recall the same material often but at various times during the learning.

Spacing effect: Achieved by introducing material over short intervals rather than one long interval.

Studying: A student process for reviewing and memorizing material.

Tenets of cooperative learning: Five conditions required for cooperative learning to be effective: (1) positive interdependence; (2) individual accountability; (3) face-to-face promotive interaction; (4) development of team skills; and (5) regular assessment of team functions.

Testing phenomenon: An experimental result that shows that retrieval events are better methods of learning than studying events.

Transfer: Using material in a situation that is different from the initial learning event.

Working memory: Generalization of short-term memory but also includes an executive processor.

References

Alba, J. W. and Hutchinson, J. W. "Knowledge Calibration: What Consumers Know and What They Think They Know." *Journal of Consumer Research*, 27, 123–156, 2000.

Amador, J. A., Miles, L., and Peters, C. B. *The Practice of Problem-Based Learning*. San Francisco: Jossey-Bass/Anker, 2006.

Angelo, T. A. and Cross, K. P. *Classroom Assessment Techniques: A Handbook for College Teachers*. San Francisco: Jossey Bass, 1993.

Atkinson, R. D. and Shiffrin, R. M. "Human Memory: A Proposed Systems and Its Control Processes." In K. W. Spence and J. T. Spence (Eds.), *The Psychology of Motivation and Motivation: Advances in Research and Theory* (Vol. 2, pp. 89–195). New York: Academic Press, 1968.

Bacon, F. *Novum Organum* (L. Jardine and M. Silverthorne, Trans.). Cambridge, England: Cambridge University Press, 2000. (Original work published 1620.)

Baddeley, A. D. "Is Working Memory Still Working?" *European Psychologist*, 7, 85–97, 2002.

Baddeley, A. D. "Working Memory: Multiple Models, Multiple Mechanisms." In H. L. Roediger, Y. Dudai, and S. M. Fitzpatrick, *Science of Memory: Concepts* (pp. 151–153). New York: Oxford University Press, 2007.

Baddeley, A. D. and Longman, D.J.A. "The Influence of Length and Frequency of Training Session on the Rate of Learning to Type." *Ergonomics*, 21, 627–635, 1978.

Bain, K. *What the Best College Teachers Do*. Boston: Harvard University Press, 2004.

Basili, P. A. and Sanford, P. J. "Conceptual Change Strategies and Cooperative Group Work in Chemistry." *Journal of Research in Science Teaching*, 28(4), 293–304, 1991.

Bassok, M. and Holyoak, K. "Interdomain Transfer Between Isomorphic Topics in Algebra and Physics." *Journal of Experimental Psychology: Learning, Memory, and Cognition*, 15, 153–166, 1989.

Besterfield-Sacre, M. E. Shuman, L. J., Wolfe, H., Atman, C. J., McGourty, J., Miller, R. L., Olds, B. M., and Rogers, G. M., "Defining the Outcomes: A Framework for EC=2000." *IEEE Transactions on Engineering Education*, 43(2), 100–110, May 2000.

Bjork, E. L. "Research on Learning as a Foundation for Curricular Reform and Pedagogy." In *Proceedings of the Reinvention Center's 2nd National Conference: Integrating Research into Undergraduate Education: The Value Added*. Washington, DC, 37–41, November 18–19, 2004.

Bjork, R. A. Cognition and Student Learning Research Grant Program— Proceedings from the Pre-Application Meeting of February 19, 2002—Bringing the Science of Cognition to Educational Research and Practice, Washington, DC. Available at http://www.ed.gov/offices/OERI/casl/casl_bjork.pdf (accessed March 31, 2009.)

Bjork, R. A. and Linn, M. C. "The Science of Learning and the Learning of Science: Introducing Desirable Difficulties." *APS Observer*, 19(3), 2006. Available at http://www.psychologicalscience.org/observer/getArticle .cfm?id=1952

Bligh, D. A. *What's the Use of Lectures?* San Francisco: Jossey-Bass, 2000.

Bloom, B. S. (Ed.), Engelhart, J. D., Furst, E. J., Hill, W. H., and Krathwohl, D. R. *Taxonomy of Educational Objectives: The Classification of Educational Goals, Handbook I: Cognitive Domain*. New York: David McKay, 1956.

Brainerd, C. J. and Reyna, V. F. "Fuzzy-Trace Theory and Memory Development." *Developmental Review*, 24, 396–439, 2004a.

Brainerd, C. J. and Reyna, V. F. "Gist Is the Grist: Fuzzy-Trace Theory and the New Intuitionism." *Developmental Review*, 4, 3–47, 2004b.

Bransford, J. D., Brown, A. L., Cocking, R. R., Donovan, S., and Pellegrino, J. W. *How People Learn, Brain Mind, Experience and School*. Washington, DC: National Academy Press, 1999.

Bransford, J. D., Brown, A. L., Cocking, R. R., Donovan, S., and Pellegrino, J. W. *How People Learn, Brain Mind, Experience and School* (exp. ed.). Washington, DC: National Academy Press, 2000.

Bransford, J. D. and Schwartz, D. "Rethinking Transfer: A Simple Proposal with Multiple Implications." *Review of Research in Education*, 24, 61–100, 1999.

Bransford, J. D. and Stein, B. S. *The IDEAL Problem Solver: A Guide for Improving Thinking, Learning and Creativity* (2nd ed.). New York: W. H. Freeman and Company, 1993.

Burson, K. A., Larrick, R., P., and Klayman, J. "Skilled or Unskilled, but Still Unaware of It: How Perceptions of Difficulty Drive Miscalibration in Relative Comparisons." *Journal of Personality and Social Psychology*, 90, 60–77, 2006.

Catterall, J. "The Arts and the Transfer of Learning." In *Critical Links: Learning in the Arts and Student Academic and Social Development*. Washington, DC: Arts Education Partnership, 2002.

Chase, W. G. and Simon, H. A. "The Mind's Eye in Chess." In W. G. Chase (Ed.), *Visual Information Processing*. New York: Academic Press, 1973.

Chi, M.T.H. and Roscoe, R. D., "The Processes and Challenges of Conceptual Change." In M. Limón and L. Mason (Eds.), *Reconsidering Conceptual Change: Issues in Theory and Practice*. Boston: Kluwer Academic Publishers, 2002.

Clark, R. C. and Mayer, R. E. *e-Learning and the Science of Instruction*. San Francisco: Pfeiffer, 2003.

Cowan, N., *Working Memory Capacity*. New York: Psychology Press, 2005.

Davis, B. G. *Tools for Teaching*. San Francisco: Jossey-Bass, 1993.

Davis, B. G. (Contributing Ed.). *Science Teaching Reconsidered.* Washington, DC: National Academy Press, 1997.

Dempster, F. N. "The Spacing Effect: A Case Study in the Failure to Apply the Results of Psychological Research." *American Psychologist,* 43(8), 627–634, 1988.

deWinstanley, P. A. and Bjork, R. A. "Successful Lecturing: Presenting Information in Ways That Engage Effective Processing." In D. F. Halpern and M. D. Hakel (Eds.), *Applying the Science of Learning to University Teaching and Beyond.* New Directions for Teaching and Learning, No. 89, 19–31, San Francisco: Jossey-Bass, 2000.

Donovan, M. S., Bransford, J. D., and Pellegrino, J. W. (Eds.). *How People Learn: Bridging Research and Practice.* Washington, DC: National Academy Press, 1999.

Druckman, D. and Bjork, R. A. (Eds.), *Learning, Remembering, Believing: Enhancing Human Performance.* Washington, DC: National Academy Press, 1994.

Dudai, Y. "Memory: It's All About Representations." In H. L. Roediger, Y. Dudai, and S. M. Fitzpatrick, *Science of Memory: Concepts.* New York: Oxford University Press, 2007.

Eichenbaum, H., "Hippocampus: Cognitive Processes and Neural Representation That Underlie Declarative Memory." *Neuron,* 44, 109–120, 2004.

Ericsson, K. A. and Kintsch, W. "Long-Term Working Memory." *Psychological Review,* 102, 211–245, 1995.

Esiobu, G. O. and Soyibo, K. "Effects of Concept and Vee Mapping Under Three Learning Modes on Students' Cognitive Achievement in Ecology and Genetics." *Journal of Research in Science Teaching,* 32, 971–995, 1995.

Felder, R. J. "Random Thoughts . . . Learning by Doing." *Chemical Engineering Education,* 37(4), 282–283, 2003.

Festinger, L., Riecken, H. W., and Schachter, S. *When Prophecy Fails*. Minneapolis: University of Minnesota Press, 1956.

Fink, L. D., *Creating Significant Learning Experiences*. San Francisco: Jossey-Bass, 2003.

Fogarty, R., Perkins, D., and Barell, J., *How to Teach for Transfer*. Palatine, IL: Skylight Publishing, 1992.

Freire, P., *Pedagogy of the Oppressed*. New York: Herder & Herder, 1970.

Gates, A. I. "Recitation as a Factor in Memorizing." *Archives of Psychology*, 6(40), 1917.

Gathercole, S. E. "Working Memory: What It Is, and What It Is Not." In H. L. Roediger, Y. Dudai, and S. M. Fitzpatrick (Eds.), *Science of Memory: Concepts*. New York: Oxford University Press, 2007.

Gentner, D. "Analogy in Scientific Discovery: The Case of Johannes Kepler." In L. Magnani and N. J. Nersessian (Eds.), *Model-Based Reasoning: Science, Technology, Values*. New York: Kluwer Academic/Plenum Publisher, 2002.

Glover, J. A. "The 'Testing' Phenomenon: Not Gone but Nearly Forgotten." *Journal of Educational Psychology*, 81, 392–399, 1989.

Gragg, C. "Because Wisdom Can't Be Told." *Harvard Alumni Bulletin*, October 19, 1940, reprinted Harvard Business School, #451–005.

Grose, T. K. "Fertile New Ground." *ASEE Prism*, pp. 46–50, Summer 2006.

Hake, R. R. "Interactive-Engagement vs. Traditional Methods: A Six-Thousand-Student Survey of Mechanics Test Data for Introductory Physics Courses." *American Journal of Physics*, 66(1), 64–74, 1998. Also available online at http://physics.indiana.edu/~sdi/ajpv3i.pdf

Halloun, I. A. and Hestenes, D. "The Initial Knowledge State of College Physics." *American Journal of Physics*, 53, 1043–1055, 1985a.

Halloun, I. A. and Hestenes, D., "Common Sense Concepts About Motion." *American Journal of Physics*, 53, 1056–1065, 1985b.

Halpern, D. and Hakel, M., "Applying the Science of Learning to University Teaching and Beyond." In *Applying the Science of Learning to University Teaching and Beyond*. New Directions for Teaching and Learning, No. 89. San Francisco: Jossey-Bass, 2002.

Halpern, D. and Hakel, M., "Applying the Science of Learning to the University and Beyond." *Change*, 35, 36–41, 2003.

Halpern, D. and Hakel, M. "How Far Can Transfer Go? Making Transfer Happen Across Physical, Temporal, and Conceptual Space." in J. P. Mestre (Ed.), *Transfer of Learning from a Modern Multidisciplinary Perspective*. Charlotte, NC: Information Age Publishing, 2005.

Harb, J. N., Terry, R. E., Hurt, P. K., and Williamson, K. J., *Teaching Through the Cycle*. Provo, UT: Brigham Young University Press, 2009.

Haskell, E. H. *Transfer of Learning: Cognition, Instruction, and Reasoning.* New York: Academic Press, 2001.

James, W. *The Principles of Psychology*. New York: Holt, 1890, Chapter 16. Available at http://psychclassics.yorku.ca/James/Principles/index.htm (accessed January 20, 2010).

Kalman, C. S. *Successful Science and Engineering Teaching in Colleges and Universities*. San Francisco: Jossey-Bass/Anker, 2006.

Kalman, C. S., Morris, S., Cotlin, C., and Gordon, R. "Promoting Conceptual Change Using Collaborative Groups in Quantitative Gateway Courses." *American Journal of Physics*, 67(S1), S45–S51, 1999.

Kang, S.H.K., McDermott, K. B., and Roediger, H. L. III, "Test Format and Corrective Feedback Modify the Effect of Testing on Long-Term Retention." *European Journal of Cognitive Psychology*, 19, 528–558, 2007.

Karpicke, J. D. and Roediger, H. L. "Repeated Retrieval During Learning Is the Key to Long-Term Retention." *Journal of Memory and Language*, 57, 151–162, 2007.

Kaufman, D. B., Felder, R. M., and Fuller, H., "Accounting for Individual Effort in Cooperative Learning Teams." *Journal of Engineering Education*, 89(2), 133–140, 2000.

Kerr, R. and Booth, B. "Specific and Varied Practice of Motor Skill." *Perceptual and Motor Skills*, 46, 395–401, 1978.

Khalifa, M. and Shen, K. N. "Effects of Knowledge Representations on Knowledge Acquisition and Problem Solving." *Electronic Journal of Knowledge Management*, 4(2), 153–158, 2006.

Kolb, D. A. *Experiential Learning Experience as a Source of Learning and Development*. Englewood Cliffs, NJ: Prentice Hall, 1984.

Kruger, J. and Dunning, D. "Unskilled and Unaware of It: How Difficulties in Recognizing One's Own Incompetence Lead to Inflated Self-Assessments." *Journal of Personality and Social Psychology*, 77(6), 1121–34, 1999.

Kuhn, T. S. *The Structure of Scientific Revolutions*. Chicago: University of Chicago Press. 1962.

Leamnson, R. *Thinking About Teaching and Learning*. Springfield, VA: Stylus, 1999.

Lionni, L. *Fish Is Fish*. New York: Alfred A. Knopf, 1974.

Lusser-Rico, G., *Writing the Natural Way: Using Right Brain Techniques to Release Your Expressive Power*. New York: Jeremy Tarcher, 1983.

Mannes S. M. and Kintsch, W. "Knowledge Organization and Text Organization." *Cognition and Instruction*, 4, 91–115, 1987.

Mayer, R. E. "Cognitive Theory and the Design of Multimedia Instruction: An Example of the Two-Way Street Between Cognition and Instruction." In D. F. Halpern and M. D. Hakel (Eds.), *Applying the Science of Learning to University Teaching and Beyond*. New Directions for Teaching and Learning Science, No. 89. San Francisco: Jossey-Bass, 2003.

Mayer, R. E. *Learning and Instruction* (2nd ed.). Upper Saddle River, NJ: Prentice-Hall, 2008.

Mazur, E. *Peer Instruction: A User's Manual.* Upper Saddle River, NJ: Prentice-Hall, 1996.

McDaniel, M. A., Anderson, J. L., Derbish, M. H., and Morrisett, N. "Testing the Testing Effect in the Classroom." *European Journal of Cognitive Psychology,* 19, 494–513, 2007.

McNamara, D. S., Kintsch, E., Songer, N. B., and Kintsch, W. "Are Good Texts Always Better? Interactions of Text Coherence, Background Knowledge, and Levels of Understanding in Learning from Text." *Cognition and Instruction,* 14(1), 1–43, 1996.

Mestre, J. *Transfer of Knowledge: Issues and Research Agenda.* Report of a workshop held at the National Science Foundation, Washington, DC, March 21–22, 2002.

Miller, G. A. "The Magical Number Seven, Plus or Minus Two: Some Limits on Our Capacity for Processing Information." *Psychological Review,* 63, 81–97, 1956.

Miller, P. H. and Bjorklund, D. "Contemplating Fuzzy Trace Theory: The Gist of It." *Journal of Experimental Child Psychology,* 71, 184–193, 1998.

Montfort, D., Brown, S., and Findley, K. "Using Interviews to Identify Student Misconceptions in Dynamics." *Proceedings of 2007 Frontiers in Education Conference, Milwaukee, WI,* 2007.

National Science Foundation. *Transfer of Knowledge: Issues and Research Agenda.* Report of a workshop held at the National Science Foundation, Washington, DC, March, 21–22, 2002.

Nissani, M. "Can the Persistence of Misconceptions Be Generalized and Explained?" *Journal of Thought,* 32(1), 69–76, 1997.

Oates, L. C. "Did Harvard Get It Right?" 59 *Mercer Law Review,* 675, 2007.

Oram, M. W. and MacLeod, M. D. "Remembering to Forget: Modeling Inhibitory and Competitive Mechanisms in Human Memory." In *Proceedings of 23rd Annual Conference Cognitive Science Society,* 738–743, 2001.

Palincsar, A. S. and Brown, A. L. "Reciprocal Teaching of Comprehension-Fostering and Comprehension-Monitoring Activities." *Cognition and Instruction*, 1, 117–175, 1984.

Pellegrino, J. W. "Rethinking and Redesigning Curriculum, Instruction and Assessment: What Contemporary Research and Theory Suggests." National Center on Education and the Economy, 2006.

Perkins, D. N. and Salomon, G. "Are Cognitive Skills Context-Bound?" *Educational Researcher*, 18(1), 16–25, 1989.

Perkins, D. N. and Salomon, G. "The Science and Art of Transfer." Harvard University Web site, 1990. http://learnweb.harvard.edu/alps/thinking/docs/trancost.pdf (accessed December 2, 2010).

Perkins, D. N. and Salomon, G. "Transfer of Learning." In T. Husen and T. N. Postlethwaite (Eds.), *The International Encyclopedia of Education* (2nd ed., vol. 11, pp. 6452–6457). Oxford, England: Pergamon, 1994.

Petty, G. *Evidence Based Teaching*. Cheltenham, United Kingdom: Nelson Thornes, 2006.

Pittsburgh Science of Learning Center (PSLC). *Robust Learning*. Available at http://www.learnlab.org/research/wiki/index.php/Robust_learning (accessed September 2010).

Preuss, P. "Industry in Ferment." *Science*, July–August 1985, 42–46.

Prince, M. "Does Active Learning Work? A Review of the Research." *Journal of Engineering Education*, 93(3), July 2004.

Reiner, M., Slotta, J. D., Chi, M.T.H., and Resnick, L. B. "Naive Physics Reasoning: A Commitment to Substance-Based Conceptions." *Cognition and Instruction*, 18(1), 1–34, 2001.

Reyna, V. "Dual Processes in Reasoning and Decision Making: Fuzzy Rationality." In *Two Minds: Dual-Process Theories of Reasoning and Rationality*. The Open University, United Kingdom, July 5–7, 2006.

Reyna, V. F. and Brainerd, C. J. "Fuzzy-Trace Theory: Some Foundational Issues." *Learning and Individual Differences*, 7, 145–162, 1995.

Reynolds, R. E., Sinatra, G. M., and Royer, J. M. *The Cognitive Revolution in Educational Psychology*. Charlotte, NC: Information Age Publishing, 2005.

Roediger, H. L. and Karpicke, J. D. "The Power of Testing Memory: Basic Research and Implications for Educational Practice." *Perspectives on Psychological Science*, 1, 181–210, 2006.

Sacks, P. *Generation X Goes to College*. Peru, IL: Open Court Publishing House, 1996.

Sadler, P. *A Private Universe* (DVD). S. Burlington, VT: Annenberg Media, 1989. Available from Annenberg MEDIAA, P.O. Box 2345, S. Burlington VT 05407-2345 and www.learner.org (Accessed Dec. 1, 2010).

Sadler, P. *Minds of Our Own* (DVD). S. Burlington, VT: Annenberg Media, 1996. Available from Annenberg MEDIA, P.O. Box 2345, S. Burlington VT 05407-2345 and www.learner.org (Accessed Dec. 1, 2010).

Salomon, G. and Perkins, D. A. "Teaching for Transfer." *Educational Leadership*, 46, 22–32, 1988.

Schacter, D. L. "Memory, Delineating the Core." In H. L. Roediger, Y. Dudai, and S. M. Fitzpatrick, *Science of Memory: Concepts* (pp. 23–27). New York: Oxford University Press, 2007.

Schroth, M. L. "Effects of Frequency of Feedback on Transfer in Concept Identification." *American Journal of Psychology*, 110(1), 71–79, 1997.

Schwartz, D. L. and Bransford J. D. "A Time for Telling." *Cognition and Instruction*, 16, 475–522, 1998.

Shank, P. "Can They Do It in the Real World? Designing for Transfer of Learning." *eLearning Developers Journal*, September 7, 2004.

Sloutsky, V. M., Kaminski, J. A., and Heckler, A. F. "The Advantage of Simple Symbols for Learning and Transfer." *Psychonomic Bulletin & Review*, 12, 508–513, 2005.

Son, L. K. "Introduction: A Metacognition Bridge." *European Journal of Cognitive Psychology*, 19, 481–493, 2007.

Son, L. K. and Vandierendonck, A. (Eds.). "Bridging Cognitive Science and Education: Learning, Memory, and Metacognition." *European Journal of Cognitive Psychology*, 19(4–5), 2007.

Sousa, D. A. *How the Brain Learns* (3rd ed.). Thousand Oaks, CA: Corwin Press, 2006.

Spence, L. D. "The Case Against Teaching." *Change*, November–December 2001.

Spitzer, H. F. "Studies in Retention." *Journal of Educational Psychology*, 30, 641–656, 1939.

Stage, F. K., Muller, P. A., Kinzie, A., and Simmons, J. *Creating Learner-Centered Classrooms: What Does Learning Theory Have to Say?* Washington, DC: ERIC Clearinghouse on Higher Education and the Association for the Study of Higher Education, 1998.

Stein, R. and Hurd, S. *Using Student Teams in the Classroom: A Faculty Guide.* Boston, MA: Anker, 2000.

Sweller, J. and Chandler, P. "Why Some Material Is Difficult to Learn." *Cognition and Instruction*, 12(3), 185–233, 1994.

Thorndike, E. L. "Mental Discipline in High School Studies." *Journal of Educational Psychology*, 15, 1–22, 1924.

Thorndike, E. L. and Woodworth, R. S. "The Influence of Improvement in the Mental Function Upon the Efficiency of Other Functions." *Psychological Review*, 8, 247–261, 1901.

Tobias, S. *Revitalizing Undergraduate Science*, Tucson, AZ: Research Corporation, 1992.

Tuckman, B. W., and Jensen, M. C. "Stages of Small-Group Development Revisited." *Group and Organization Studies*, 2(4), 419, 1977.

Turns, J., Atman, C., and Adams, R. "Concept Maps for Engineering Education: A Cognitively Motivated Tool Supporting Varied Assessment Functions." *IEEE Transactions on Education*, 32(2), 164–173, 2000.

University of Memphis. "Practice at Retrieval." http://www.psyc.memphis.edu/learning/principles/lp3.shtml (accessed September 2009).

Vosniadou, S. and Brewer, W. F. "Mental Models of the Earth: A Study of Conceptual Change in Childhood." *Cognitive Psychology*, 24, 535–585, 1992.

Wankat, P. C. *The Effective, Efficient Professor: Teaching, Scholarship and Service.* Boston, MA: Allyn & Bacon, 2002.

Weimer, M., *Learner-Centered Teaching.* San Francisco: Jossey-Bass, 2002.

Wiggins, G. and McTighe, J., *Understanding by Design.* Upper Saddle River, NJ: Prentice-Hall, 2001.

Wolfe, C. R., Reyna, V. F., and Brainerd, C. J. "Fuzzy-Trace Theory: Implications for Transfer in Teaching and Learning." In J. P. Mestre, *Transfer of Learning from a Modern Multidisciplinary Perspective*. Charlotte, NC: Information Age Publishing, 2005.

Woods, D. R. *Problem-Based Learning: How to Gain the Most from PBL.* Hamilton, ON: W. L. Griffin Printing, 1994.

Woods, D. R. "Issues in Implementation in an Otherwise Conventional Program." In D. Boud and G. Feletti (Eds.), *The Challenge of Problem-Based Learning* (Chapter 17). London: Kogan Page, 2001.

Zola-Morgan, S. and Squire, L. R. "The Primate Hippocampal Formation: Evidence for a Time-Limited Role in Memory Storage." *Science*, 250, 288–289, 1990.

Index

Page references followed by *fig* indicate an illustrated figure; followed by *t* indicate a table.